10 THINGS YOU NEED TO KNOW ABOUT LAND

A HOW-TO GUIDE ABOUT
LOTS AND VACANT LAND
FOR AGENTS, INVESTORS, AND YOU!

CHERYL L. SAIN
Licensed Real Estate Broker & US Veteran

10 Things You Need to Know About Land: A How-To Guide
About Lots and Vacant Land for Agents, Investors, and You!
White Hawk LLC, Matthews, NC 28104

This publication is designed to provide competent and reliable information regarding the subject matter covered in this guide. It is sold with the understanding that author and publisher are not engaged in rendering legal, professional, or financial advice. Laws, regulations, and practices vary from state to state and county to county, if legal or other expert advice is required, the services of a professional should be investigated and searched out. The author and publisher specifically disclaim any liability that is incurred from the use or application of the contents of this book.

This information is provided as-is and does not in any way make or imply any guarantees as to an outcome. You will need to evaluate the information herein and consult appropriate professionals such as surveyors, attorneys, tax accountants, or any other professional agencies or broker-in-charge to acquire the information and guidance you need to help you make the decision that is best for you.

ISBN: 978-1-7353023-4-8

Edited by: Lindsey Alexander

Published by: Warren Publishing
Charlotte, NC
www.warrenpublishing.net

Printed in the United States

"Cheryl Sain's book is absolutely required reading for all investors and real estate brokers, in my opinion. My hope is you will enjoy, learn, and refer to her book for many years to come in your personal and professional purchasing and selling of commercial and residential property. As a real estate broker myself, a broker-in-charge, an educator, and a school director and owner for thirty-six years, I believe Cheryl's book and concepts taught in the classroom or online would be phenomenal for students!"

–Bill Gallagher, DREI, GRI
Founder, Superior School of Real Estate

"I used to think that most of the best brokers wouldn't share their secrets, but after reading Cheryl's book, I now know that the best do share and can do it very well! If you are seeking a primer to land brokerage, this is a book that will give you a foundation to transact with confidence."

–John Culbertson CCIM, CRE, SIOR,
Cardinal Real Estate Partners, LLC

"Representing real estate in today's market requires a considerable knowledge of applicable laws, markets, science, zoning, community master plans, etc. Before Cheryl drafted this book, I knew of no single source reference that helped agents look in the right direction for the answer they needed. This book will be a "go-to" reference for many new and experienced agents."

–Richard L. Harmon, PG, Harmon Environmental, PA

"Before anyone decides to engage in a business transaction involving land, this is a MUST-READ book. You will find that taking the time to drill down these ten facts about land will preserve a successful transaction where the end result will be a win-win. If I had had access to this book when I initially began my professional career, it would have prevented my learning the hard way."

–Cisco Garcia, PE, MASCE
AMH Development, Regional Vice President of Operations

"With this book, Cheryl has put together an easy-to-read reference for anyone dealing with land transactions. Her experience in the real estate industry and desire to assemble information, never before put together in a single source, makes this a must-have for any landowner or real estate professional."

–Tim Bowes, PLS, Geomatics Manager
2019 President North Carolina Society of Surveyors
VHB Engineering NC, PC

"This book is full of important information for those of us who want to enjoy the companionship of first-hand knowledge based on experience from Ms. Sain. She will take you from A–Z in this real estate book, and what you need to know".

–Kenneth Owens, NC Real Estate Broker, NC Licensed Soil Scientist, NC Subsurface Operator, NC Septic Inspector, SC Professional Soil Classifier, and President and Owner of Septic Environmental Solutions, Inc.

Dedication

I dedicate this part of my life's work to my parents, Gene and Catherine Sain, who have been the source of my greatest support and endless encouragement. Your unconditional love and kindness have been a shining light that guided me through life's challenges, and you were a constant reminder of God's love for us all. Your positive attitude and endless generosity have served as an exceptional example for how to treat others: *Just be nice*. You have said many times that I can do whatever I put my mind to and efforts in. I can have whatever I want if I am willing to work for it. These cherished life lessons are part of the fabric of who I have become. Thank you for being my parents and reflecting examples of everything good.

To my three beautiful children, who are the loves of my life: I am forever grateful for all the laughter and joy you have brought me throughout the years. I am so very proud of the young adults each of you have become. I love you all. As I often say, "Conner, you are my favorite oldest child; Jake, you are my favorite middle child; and Emma, you are my favorite daughter." Always stay true to your values and never compromise your convictions.

Most of all, I want to thank the Lord who has been my constant guide and love. I thank Him for placing me in positions to help others achieve their goals and to share smiles and laughter with all those whom I have the privilege of serving.

To everyone who reads this book, let me share one of my favorite quotes:

"Be good to people.
You will be remembered more for
your kindness than any level of success
you could possibly attain."[1]

–MANDY HALE,
NEW YORK TIMES BEST-SELLING AUTHOR

“On the extra mile, it’s mostly an open road, and that is where all the difference is made.”

–Cheryl Sain

Contents

"Hauling and hoping, driving and showing, praying and pitching, sitting and wishing, listing and selling."[2]

–Bill Gallagher,
Real Estate Agent, Broker in Charge and Educator

Introduction

How many of you real estate agents in North and South Carolina have heard those words from Bill Gallagher, one of the funniest real estate educators in the industry? I know I have heard it dozens of times, and it still makes me laugh! If you are a residential real estate agent, you know this saying to be true. The same can be said for land brokers. We've all spent hours drudgingly going through each of these steps. Sometimes it pays off; sometimes it doesn't.

Having been involved in real estate in North and South Carolina since 2001, my primary focus has been land sales. Throughout my career, I have encountered many residential agents/brokers, investors, and landowners who simply do not understand the land aspects of real estate. I've spent many hours on the phone with agents and landowners explaining information about parcels of land. All too often, residential real estate professionals believe land deals are too complicated and difficult to understand. But are they really? There's a common expression that says, "Sometimes you just don't know what you don't know!" Writing this book is my way of helping others learn in a short amount of time what took me years to learn.

During my research for this book, I was unable to find any other source that actually assembles the basics of what you need to know and where to find it with regards to land. While I was in the process of writing this book, successful land developers told me they wished they'd had this type of reference material when they had first started out in their careers. Likewise, I think you, too, will appreciate the value as you go through each chapter and begin to apply what you learn to your land dealings. The information you now hold in your hands will save hours of research because you will know where to find the information you need for successful and timely land transactions or just for your own personal knowledge of your land.

The motivation for developing this book came from the struggles I encountered when I started out in the real estate industry. I want to save you the time it took me to learn all of these things so you can get started helping others, or yourself, buy and sell land!

REMEMBER: You are the best investment you can make! You just took an important next step to further your knowledge of land sales. This book is for everyone who has anything to do with land. Whether you have a house on land, inherited land, invest in land, or buy or sell land, this is for you! After reading this book, you will have a more thorough understanding of researching land, which will give you an advantage in the real estate field as well as allow you to assist others—clients, friends, or family. By remembering and practicing these ten simple steps, your knowledge of land will increase considerably.

My goal was to make this reference material simple and easy to read to gain basic information and provide motivation. I hope *10 Things You Need to Know About Land* will become part of your desk library for your daily use and source of encouragement. I believe this book will help enhance your knowledge before you list, sell, or purchase land. Read through it. Mark up the pages. Tab items of interest. Carry it with you. Make it your own!

Now let's get started doing real good things, today!

“Don’t be intimidated by what you don’t know. That can be your greatest strength and ensure that you do things differently from everyone else.”[3]

–Sara Blakely, Founder and CEO of Spanx

"Under all is the land."[4]

–Arthur Barnhisel, 1924 Chair of the NAR Ethics Committee and Author of the Preamble for the Code of Ethics

1
How to Find Land Using the GIS

Understanding how to find land has probably been the biggest asset to my career. Not only did it catapult my real estate success, but it also helped me gain recognition in the industry among my peers. Additionally, knowing how to research land put me a step ahead of my competitors. Was there a learning curve? Oh yeah!

For many years I have worked with a number of regional and national builders and local developers locating anything from one lot to an apartment site to a several-hundred-acre site for a residential neighborhood. Throughout this book, I will include some stories based on my previous experiences, so you can get an idea how I've learned to help others buy and sell land. Below, I've included one that takes you through my typical day.

Story: The willing one ...

While working with a residential home builder, I was asked to locate a parcel of land for a future multi-family commercial development. Using a vital tool called the Geographic Information System (GIS), I quickly located what appeared to be several potential parcels of vacant land in the requested location. I then began to research the land conditions through this website and acquired necessary information that I needed to get started. I narrowed it down to two parcels that met the builder's checklist. Fortunately, both parcels of land were in the path of growth and had potential to rezone for higher density (which will be explained in forthcoming chapters). Once the builder approved the locations, I then reached out to the owners of the two parcels. One of the landowners was willing to sell their land, and the other was not interested at the time. This project went under contract with the willing landowner and the builder closed.

NOTE: Occasionally I check in with the owner who was not interested in selling at that time; there may come a future opportunity for selling that person's property. You never know.

So how can you get started identifying land for your buyers? My advice is to learn everything you can about the GIS. I've included as much information as I can here to get you started.

1. Where do you start, and what is the GIS?

The geographic information system (GIS) websites are the best places to start when researching a parcel of land or property. They contain most of the parcel details you will need all in one place.

These websites analyze and display geographically referenced information readily available to the public. These websites provide spatial information (geographic locations and boundaries), soil data if available, and tabular information (data that links to the spatial data) available about a piece of land. If you are not already using it, it is about to become your new best friend.

You can access any local GIS website through most county websites if it is available in that county. You can locate the GIS site for which you are searching by typing the name of the county followed by "GIS" into any search engine.[5]

Example: "Mecklenburg County GIS"

GIS websites vary from county to county and state to state, so you may have to learn several different ones depending on the number of counties that you service. Some rural counties use a hosting entity and do not have a GIS office/department. You can find out who the hosting entity is by contacting the planning department for that county's governmental office.

Do yourself a favor and familiarize yourself with the local GIS and learn how to maneuver through the site. Experimenting with the GIS sites is the best way

to learn. Start out practicing with your own address. If you get confused, contact the GIS department for the site you are working with and ask for help. Occasionally, I still call them myself when I get hung up trying to figure out a site I am unfamiliar with. They can be very helpful, and you can establish a contact with someone in that department whom you can call from time to time.[6]

2. How do you find the county?

In order to locate the proper GIS, you will first need to determine the county in which the parcel lies. There are a few ways to locate a county. The easiest method is to enter the zip code into the browser on your computer. The information returned should tell you the city and county for that postal code.

Another method is to visit the National Association of Counties website (www.NACO.org). Once on the site, simply click on the "What We Do" tab, scroll down to the "Find a County" tab, then enter the zip code in the website search bar.

3. What can you find on the GIS?

To simply find the location of a property, click on the map to find data with the information tab, or you can call or visit the local tax office. However, the quickest and easiest way to gather information on a property is by using the GIS to locate the following:

Parcel identification number (parcel ID number or PIN)

A parcel ID number is a number each county assigns to a piece of land to identify that particular parcel. Once you are on the GIS website, type in the search tab the address of the parcel, and it will display the map of the parcel along with the property report.

Parcel address

On the other hand, the parcel ID number can help you obtain the parcel address. If you do not have the address, owner name, or PIN, it is possible to search the closest known address or landmark near the property to narrow your search. Work through the map from there until you are able to locate the parcel for which you are searching.

> **NOTE:** Not all parcels have an address! Some counties will not assign an address until a structure has been built on the property. However, all parcels will have a parcel ID number.

Owner's name

You will need either a PIN or an address to look up a parcel to find the owner's name. Typically, in the search bar for a GIS site, there will be an area for you to input what information you already have to do a search. Sometimes there will be a drop-down arrow in the search box for you to select how you would like to research, and other times it is lightly highlighted with "Enter address/parcel/owner/landmark" for you to just enter the information you have. There may be three or four ways to enter information depending on the site:

- owner's name
- parcel ID number
- address
- landmarks

Once information is entered and you click the search bar, the map should appear on the screen to show the parcel. An information sheet or property report will pop up usually at the bottom of the page or on either side of the map, depending on the site. This information sheet has all the parcel information available to you. Just scroll down the information page to see what they will allow you to discover about that particular parcel.

Typical subcategories available for a GIS parcel

Since information varies by GIS websites across the country, it is hard to say exactly how the information will display on each site. The GIS sites that I typically use are easy to navigate and user friendly. They often will include:

- **Number of acres** in a parcel.
- **Purchase date** of property (most recent available).
- **Purchase amount**—In states that require disclosure, the purchase amount may be found in the deed. Also, this is typically available through the tax assessor's office. If only the deed stamps (taxes) amount is available, the tax multiplier for the state helps

to determine the purchase amount. The tax assessor's office can provide the rate of the stamps (taxes) and how to convert it into a sales price. More information can be found by visiting: https://finance.zacks.com/taxable-deed-stamp-7284.html.

- **Zoning**—A designation that shows the county's current allowable use of the land.
- **Property boundary**—In the GIS, it is a mapping display of boundary property lines that define the lay of the land and features of the surface of the land.
- **Topography**—Contour lines that define the lay of the land with elevations that can include site features such as rivers, streams, ponds, lakes, etc.[7]
- **Aerial**—A photo image of the property from above (it might not be current).
- **Easements**—Illustrations on the map that show recorded accesses through or to the property. These may show up as utilities, roads, and driveways, to name a few.
- **Utility locations**—Utility easements on or near the property illustrated on the map.
- **Water features and flood plain/zone areas**—Illustrations in this layer may show streams, ponds, lakes, and rivers on or near a property, and the image layer can show if a property is close to water and could be subject to flooding. This can only be determined by a survey.

- **Soil information**—Soil types and locations.
- Details on adjacent properties.

These are a few of the basic things you can find on the GIS website. Much more information is available once you spend some time learning how to maneuver through the site.

If you want to learn a detailed GIS system, check out the Environmental Systems Research Institute website, www.esri.com. This program is called ArcGIS. The program has a steep learning curve, but it might be fun for you techies. The GIS will give you more mapping information than you might ever need.

> **NOTE:** Although GIS websites are full of valuable information, they might not be current. GIS sites are not updated daily, or even weekly—so double-check the information through the county Register of Deeds. Some counties might update only every few months. A property might have sold just the week before, been transferred to a different family member, or be in foreclosure. Many different scenarios affect a property and its information on the GIS, so do your homework.
>
> Additionally, you should confirm your findings with a recorded survey and deed with the appropriate county departments. For me personally, the GIS is still my go-to when initially researching land.

Now that we've gone over the basic information you can find on the GIS, take a moment to locate the GIS website for your area and spend some time exploring it so you, too, can learn how to use this resource. You will find yourself coming back again

and again as this becomes the starting point for most property searches. After you've found what you can on the GIS, you will feel much more confident as you do further research on possible locations for your buyers and gather information for your sellers about their property.

"You cannot change your destination overnight, but you can change your direction overnight."[8]

–Jim Rohn

"The question is not what you look at, but what you see."[9]

–Henry David Thoreau

Finding Parcel Owners' Names and Addresses

Story: The property they didn't own ... or did they?

I have a client named Eduardo who occasionally asks me to help him with finding homes to purchase that he can rent out. On one particular occasion, he asked me to check on a vacant house located on a road he travels daily. He believed the house to be abandoned as it was overgrown with vegetation and there never seemed to be any vehicles there.

After driving to the property to see for myself, I realized he was correct. The property was a mess. The windows were all broken, the electrical had been stripped from the walls, the doors smashed, and vines were growing into the house. The good things were

that the house had a brick veneer, the roof was in good enough shape to prevent leaks, there seemed to be no significant settlement cracks, the structure of the house looked to be solid, and, to boot, it was situated on more than an acre of land. So, my buyer asked if I could research the house and owners to determine details about the property and if they would be interested in selling.

I went to work researching through the GIS website and through tax records. I located an investment group in New York that at one time owned a portfolio of houses in the state. This particular vacant house was one of them. The group claimed they no longer owned any houses in that state and that I must be mistaken. At that point, I suggested they take a look at the research data I had compiled along with the recent photos showing the current condition of the house. I sent them everything I'd compiled. Through reviewing my work plus their own internal research, they realized that they did still own this one remaining house.

We sent them an offer to purchase, which they eventually accepted. As the house had been vandalized and abandoned, there was much work to make it habitable again. Once renovations were completed, Eduardo added yet another property to his rental inventory.

"The difference between try and triumph is a little umph."[10]

–Marvin Phillips

Below you'll find a list of my methods for finding and contacting owners of a property along with tips for successful communication.

1. Who are the legal owners of a parcel?

It is important to find the correct person or people to speak with regarding ownership of a property. You can find all of this information either on the GIS or from the tax assessor's office. Give your local tax assessor's office a call and have an address or parcel ID number ready; this will make the process go a little faster. I will start out with, "I am a real estate agent researching a property. Can you please help me locate some information about a parcel?" I give them the information I have to help the assessor locate the parcel in question. Sometimes I just say, "What can you tell me about the parcel?"

Often these days I have a more difficult time locating an owner mainly because most people have cell phones now instead of house phones. In one particular situation I had to contact a neighbor who, luckily, gave me the elderly owners' children's names and happened to have their phone numbers on hand. In another instance, I had to search for people with the same last name near the subject to see if they were related and could share the relative's contact information. Just keep asking questions.

Here is an example of how I do it. "Hey," I say, and because I am southern I add, "my name is Cheryl and I am trying to locate Mr. or Mrs. Smith who owns the property located on blah blah back road.

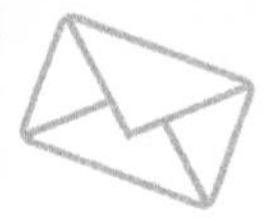

I am having trouble reaching them; is it possible you are a relative? Can you please help me contact them? Maybe you have a current phone number? Or do you know their immediate relatives?" Sometimes they will only have enough information to help you start down another search trail. Another question might be, "Do you happen to know where they work?" This question has helped me many times over the years.

2. How many owners are there?

There may be several owners, but they may elect one person to represent and negotiate. To be certain, ask who is handling the property or representing the owners. Confirm this representative with all of the parties involved and make certain that they all agree with the decisions made by the representative. It is a little more work, but it is better to be certain going into a deal than to have it fall apart because all parties are not in agreement.

3. How do I contact the owners?

You can find the mailing addresses through the tax assessor's office as well as on the GIS under the property information card/tab. Some GIS websites call it a property report. Other methods when trying to make contact with the owner might include:

- using "People Search" websites
- asking neighbors of the property in question for additional contact information
- contacting the HOA if the property is within a homeowners association

- browsing professional websites or social media
- my old-fashioned favorite, writing a personal letter using the address on the tax records. I may type the letter, but I will certainly put my signature at the bottom of the letter and hand write the address on the envelope. This gives it a more personal feel and shows that it wasn't spit out by a computer in a mass mailing.

> **NOTE:** The owners are not necessarily listed as the contact for the property. The contact person could be an attorney or an agent or a family representative (for example, the executor of the estate).

4. How do you find contact information for an entity or business owner through the secretary of state's (SOS) website?

If the property owner is an entity or business, you might be able to look up their contact information on the secretary of state's website for the state where the property is located. To locate the secretary of state's website, type the state name for where the property is located followed by "Secretary of State."

Example: "North Carolina Secretary of State."

> **NOTE:** Some secretary of state websites charge a fee for the information.

Once on the site, find the corporation search page. Enter the entity or business name and the results should display the owners or agent representative and a phone number. You might have to go back to the original filings (the date when they first registered the entity

or business) to get the owner or agent representative information. This could require a phone call to the secretary of state's office in the state in which you are researching. The contact person for the property might be an agent representative for the owner, such as an attorney or a legal family representative.

After you have located an owner and discovered that they might be interested in selling, you will need as much information about the parcel as they can provide. Any information you can get from the owner of the property is helpful, but you will always need to verify the facts. Ask the property owner questions that make them feel comfortable discussing the property—they will talk. Listen and learn. The following chapter will give you a list of many items you may want to cover with an owner.

“Try not to become a person of success, but rather try to become a person of value.”[11]

–Albert Einstein

"Land is the only thing in the world that amounts to anything."[12]

–Margaret Mitchell,
Gone with the Wind

Discovering Land Conditions

Story: The "hot mess" property

Linda, a client of mine, had been keeping an eye on a house for sale in a neighborhood she liked. She asked me to check it out for her, so as her real estate professional, I went through the usual research and pulled up the information on the local multiple listing service (MLS). As I was reading the information in the comment section, red flags started waving on the screen (figuratively speaking). When I read, "sold strictly as-is using a quit claim deed" and "please talk to your attorney about this type of deed," I knew this property had major issues that would have to be addressed.

Using the GIS to further research the property for the aerial view and property layout, I was very surprised at the findings. This property was a hot

mess. According to the GIS aerial, the property line for the adjacent property ran directly through the house Linda was interested in buying. After a long explanation to Linda of what I believed it might take to get this legal property line mess resolved, not to mention the amount of time and money involved, she asked me what I would do if I were in her shoes. Honestly, my initial instinct was, "Run … and don't look back!" However, I said to Linda, "If you decide to move forward, I would start with a survey!" And no, Linda did not move forward with a purchase on this property, just so you know. She actually moved out of state to be near her aging mother. But the experience reminded me that taking the time to research land conditions before making an offer saves everyone a lot of hassle.

And by the way, the agent could not get that house sold; he dropped the listing and told me it truly was a "hot mess."

> **NOTE:** If you are an agent and have a situation similar to this one mentioned in the hot mess story, where the client wants to continue moving forward, do yourself a favor and have the client sign a statement (waiver) affirming that you explained and disclosed the situation thoroughly and it was the client's decision to continue to move forward. You'll be glad you did later on. Also, keep in mind that GIS lot lines are frequently inaccurate, which is why a survey is the best place to start.

Image is author's own.

The GIS shows property lines going through the structure, creating a hot mess indeed.

Discovering the conditions of a property early on is imperative when deciding how, when, or if you will move forward with a property. By uncovering issues in the beginning, such as what happened with Linda, you can save yourself a lot of time and headaches on a property that may have resulted in an undesirable situation. Do your homework and learn as much as possible on the front end of a transaction to facilitate a smoother transition from one owner to another. Knowing everything from mortgages and liens to stormwater runoff and everything in between is essential to qualifying the land for a successful transaction.

If your client is interested in buying a parcel that may not be listed or if you have another client who

is interested in selling their property, there are things you need to know in order to move forward. If you are establishing a working relationship with a seller, there are a few things you need to know up front, and asking certain questions may feel awkward. The first thing I do is talk casually with the owners to get to know them and for them to get comfortable with me. I try to find common interests to build rapport. I then kindly say, “May I ask you some questions about your property?” (Don’t rush! Take a southern minute to get to know them, and it will go a long way.) What is that saying by Teddy Roosevelt? “Nobody cares how much you know until they know how much you care.”[13] I have found this quote to be so true. People are funny about their land; some are very sentimental, while others are just about the money. You need to figure out what type of person you are working with early on to help you negotiate better.

Some of the following questions may strike a nerve, so try to phrase the question in a manner that is gentle and curious-sounding rather than, as Joe Friday says, “just the facts, ma’am.” If the client is going through a foreclosure, you can bet they are sensitive; try to be aware of his or her body language when asking the initial questions. This will help you out tremendously as you gather information about the property.

Other clients may be property flippers and it is just a financial transaction for them. They mainly want to know how you can make them money, so this may be a time for you to show your stuff, meaning how great of an agent you really are and that you can get the job done and done well. Just don’t spend too

much time talking about yourself and your resume. Investors really just want to know what you can do for them; they typically don't care what you have done for someone else. I know that sounds harsh, but it is the gospel truth.

The following talking points are critical in moving forward.

1. Mortgages, liens, and title issues

Mortgages

Are there any mortgages or deeds of trust on the property? Find this information in the register of deeds office at the county courthouse. Many counties now have online lookup available, but some may charge a fee for the online access.

Liens

Are there any liens on the property that the owner is aware of? A lien on real estate is when a creditor attaches a notice to the property claiming the owner owes money to the creditor. This is a way for them to collect what they are owed when a property changes ownership. You can typically find this information by contacting your local county tax assessor's office and the register of deeds office, or it should be noted in a title search.[14]

Title issues

Is the owner aware of any title issues? If the property does not have a clear chain of title—for example, outstanding liens—what would those be? A closing

attorney or a title company can find this out when they have a title search performed. Unpaid taxes could also prevent a clear title.

Taxes

Are there unpaid or back taxes? A title search will also uncover any unpaid or back taxes. If there is an outstanding tax balance that is owed, it is typically taken out of the seller's proceeds at closing, or the seller could request the buyer contribute funds in payment of delinquent taxes.

How will the tax rate affect the property? There are different tax considerations when purchasing raw land than when purchasing land with a structure. Consider the implication on the property after it is improved. You don't want to be surprised with a large unplanned or unexpected annual tax bill. Contact the tax assessor's office to confirm the taxes on the property as well as the tax rate of the parcel as-is, versus if built upon or with improvements.

Rollback-taxes

Often agricultural land receives exemptions or a reduced rate of taxes on the property taxes due. These reduced rates are considered deferred taxes. When a property changes its use, let's say from agricultural to residential or commercial use, then the tax assessor's office determines the amount due and will go back a period of time—in some states, typically three to five years—to collect the deferred taxes. This deferred tax payment is a one-time payment and is the responsibility of the seller or owner of the property

but sometimes can be negotiated between a buyer and seller. Who is responsible to pay the rollback taxes should be stated in the sales contract.

> **NOTE:** Taxes differ depending on the use of the land. For example, investment properties may be taxed at a higher amount because they are income-producing. Check with your local tax assessor's office to confirm tax rates for the property you have interest in.

Foreclosure

Is the property currently under foreclosure or in a pre-foreclosure situation? Properties go into foreclosure for a variety of reasons. This is important to know because there may be conditions and/or restrictions that need to be discovered prior to a purchase. You can also find this information at the register of deeds office at the courthouse.

2. Appraisals

Have you had a recent appraisal on the property? An appraisal is a valuation or assessment of property. It establishes a property's market value or what the property would bring if offered for sale in the real estate market or for taxation purposes. These appraisals are detailed reports compiled by a licensed appraiser typically selected by the lender, individual, or entity interested in an appraisal.

Lenders will require an appraisal when a home buyer uses the home for security for their mortgages. The appraisal provides the lender with the assurance that the property is worth at least what the mortgage company is lending on it. However, an individual

or business owner considering selling their property may hire an appraiser to evaluate the property prior to a sale to ensure they are pricing it properly by understanding its current value. Appraisals can also be a helpful tool in resolving conflicts between heirs to an estate by establishing the value of the real estate or personal property to be divided.

Who pays for an appraisal? Typically, the buyer. However, it could be negotiated upfront to be paid by the seller or you could consider using a broker price opinion.[15]

3. Deed restrictions, easements, and access

Deed restrictions

Are there any deed restrictions on the property? A deed restriction is a provision in a deed that limits what can and cannot be built on a property and how the property can or cannot be used. Deed restrictions run with the land—meaning the restrictions in the deed apply to all future owners of the property if the property is sold. Deed restrictions are private land use controls, as opposed to zoning laws, which are public land use controls.

Thoroughly read through the deed to discover any restrictions. You can get a copy of the deed from the county register of deeds office for the property you are researching. Any deed restrictions are typically stated in the legal description. The county staff will need the parcel ID number (see chapter one) or the address of the parcel to look up the deed for you.[16]

> **NOTE:** Legal descriptions are not the same thing as a parcel ID number. Tax parcel IDs and PINs are NOT legal descriptions; they are reference tax records.

Buried Items

Are there any buried items on the property? Sometimes things are buried on a property that the current owner may or may not be aware of. Buried items, if any, could affect the soils and the ability to use the soils for building purposes. You might need a specialist to remove old farm equipment, debris burial pits, USTs (underground storage tanks used for old oil furnaces), oil or gas tanks, or bad soils (just to name a few) and refill the land with clean soil if necessary.

Depending on the planned use of the land, a Phase 1 Environmental Site Assessment (ESA) might be necessary. The local/regional department of environmental quality or a hired consultant of a group should be able to discover potential problems that could be expensive to remedy.

A Phase 1 ESA is a historical document review of both the site and surrounding properties. It will identify possible environmental issues on or near the site that could affect the sale or use of the land. It is better to find this out early in the transaction rather than later down the line when money has been spent on site layouts, planning, and (possibly) engineer involvement. This is the responsibility of the buyer. However, a diligent real estate agent may suggest this to be completed early on in the process. If performed properly, a Phase 1 ESA will indemnify a buyer from any environmental liability.[17]

Cemeteries

Are you aware of any type of cemeteries or burial grounds on the property? Most states have strict laws regarding cemeteries and sacred burial grounds. You should research your particular state's laws in this case. If you own or inherit land that has a known cemetery or burial site, you will especially need to know the laws as you consider preparing a property for transfer of ownership now or in the future. Likewise, if you are considering purchasing a property that has a designated cemetery or burial ground on it, know that it will have a restricted use. It can be a very expensive and, possibly, long process to relocate a burial ground.

Easements

Do you know of any kind of easements on the property? An easement gives someone legal access to property they do not own—such as road access or utility lines. Some utility easements are obvious, and some are not. A current survey should show easements such as power, sewer, water, and gas lines, among others. Additionally, a deed will describe a road or driveway easement that may not appear on a survey. There are other types of easements that are not so obvious.

View easement

Is there a view easement for this property? Yes, this is a real thing! You might not think about a view easement unless you are considering a property with

a mountain, water, or even city view. These types of easements must be taken seriously and be well-researched prior to closing on a lot or parcel or even an existing home. For example, some of the restrictions or limitations affecting a view could be:

- Trees that would block a view for another property owner
- Removing trees that could expose an unsightly view or diminish someone's privacy
- Adding a structure on the part of the property that could block a view
- Restrictions on size and height of a structure

When purchasing or selling a property that is marketed "with a view," it is imperative to make certain that the view is protected by including it in the deed and that you understand the existing restrictions.

> **NOTE:** Remember that a title search should address easement concerns.

Seasonal views

As with the view easements, this, too, is something to consider when researching a property or lot. When you are looking at a parcel or lot, you will want to consider times of the year when the leaves are on or off the trees and whether the view is still what you expect it to be.

Landlocked property

Is there a legally documented access to the property? Landlocked property is a piece of property that is surrounded by other properties and has no access

to the closest road. Before you consider buying or selling a landlocked property, determine whether the property has road access. This can be accomplished by obtaining a current survey to know exactly what you are dealing with.

Access

Does the property provide legal access to a public road? Where is the land in relation to a road? If the property sits behind another property that has road access and/or frontage, does a legal, recorded document give a road-access easement to the property you are considering? This, too, can be accomplished by obtaining a current survey to find accessibility to the land.

> **NOTE**: This is very important. You might want to think twice before purchasing or trying to list a property for sale that is landlocked unless you are sure that access is covered under the title policy and/or deed. You might have to approach the adjacent landowner to see if they will allow an easement on or through their property prior to closing.

Weather access

What is the access plan to and from the property during inclement weather? You might want to consider the access for year-round living on a property. If you have a property in a mountainous area, you will want to take into account how you will be able to access the property during inclement weather conditions. The same might be true for the beach areas where island resorts or homes use a bridge to access the property.

4. Air rights

Does the property have an air rights situation? The property interest in the vertical space above the earth's surface is referred to as "air rights." Air rights permit developing the empty airspace above a physical property site/location. As with other types of real estate, an owner can transfer the ownership of this airspace to others while retaining ownership of the physical property itself. Skywalks, skyways, sky bridges, or other elevated types of pedestrian crosswalks between buildings, typically in urban areas, are just a few examples.[18, 19] These are managed and maintained by private owners while some are publicly owned by federal or state governments. In order for air rights to be valid, they must be in a deed.[20]

5. Mineral, oil, and gas rights

Are the mineral, oil, and gas rights still attached to the property? The rights to minerals, oils, or gases that could be extracted from the property are often sold or leased to businesses or individuals. This is called mining. If the property contains natural resources, you should make sure the rights are intact with the land and not sold or leased out prior to a land purchase. This will be discussed in more detail in chapter seven.

6. Drones

Has the property ever been surveyed with drone photography? A drone is an unmanned aircraft or unmanned aerial vehicle (UAV). Drones range in

size depending on your needs and are navigated remotely. These drones are equipped with cameras for photography or videos.

Is drone photography necessary for real estate? As many in today's real estate market know, how you market a property can make all the difference in piquing a potential buyer's interest. Over the past few years, drones have become almost an assumed way to market a property or piece of land.

Realtors hire a drone pilot to take aerial photos or videos of a property for marketing purposes. These resources are especially effective in hard-to-access areas or in showing a large property, its location, and (possibly) surrounding areas.

To find a professional drone pilot in your area, just type "Licensed drone pilots in (your city)" in the search engine of your choice. You will want to be sure to hire a drone pilot licensed and insured under the FAA's Small Unmanned Aircraft Regulations (also known as "Part 107") for their expertise in drone photography services. These licensed drone pilots are aware of the rules and regulations associated with filming property, people, and public buildings, and of airspace violations. Hobby and recreational drone use is different from business or commercial use; do not confuse the two.[21]

7. Topography

What exactly is topography? Topography (topo) is the mapping or charting of the shape and features of the land using contour lines. Each contour line follows

specific elevations, thereby showing the curvature of the terrain and the presence of hills and valleys. A topographic map of the land will show whether the land is flat or has rolling hills, or the height and shape of mountains and water features. The topography of the parcel of land will help determine for what the property can be used and if it is suitable for structures to be built. For example, if the property is too steep, it might not be good for a residential neighborhood but good for livestock farming or some other use not requiring level terrain.

Do you know the topography of the property? A landowner may or may not have a topographic map of the property on hand. A quick glimpse of the topography can be accessed on most GIS websites. Depending on the GIS website you are using, the topography information might be under different tabs labeled "Layers," "Contours," or "Topo." The property maps might look great on an aerial layer; however, you might turn on the multiple layers on the GIS and discover the land is unbuildable because of the topography. Potential buyers and investors are wise to hire a surveyor to complete a more detailed and current analysis of the property before considering a development of any kind.

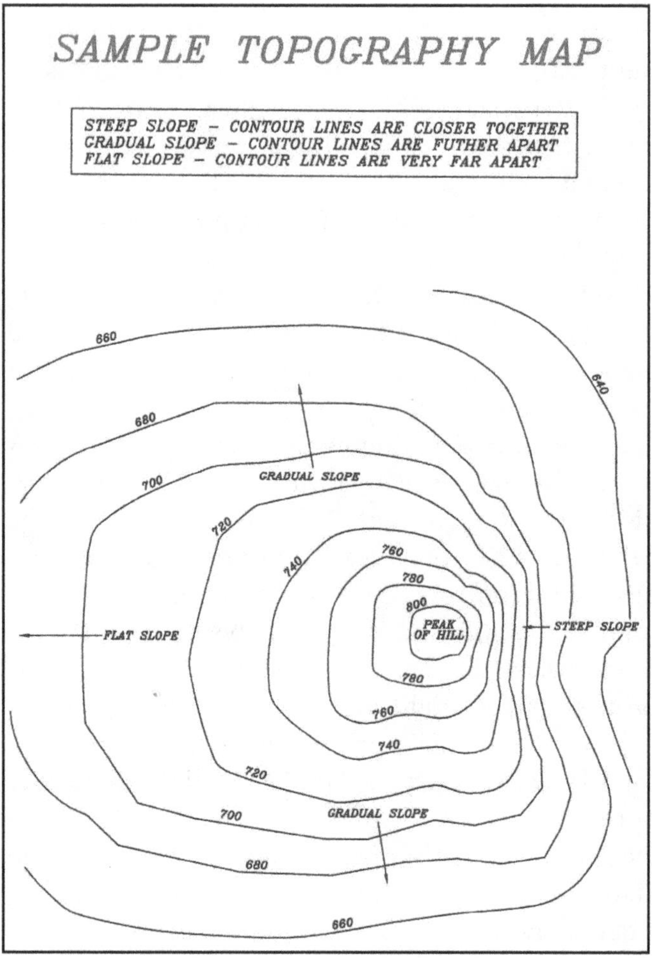

SAMPLE TOPOGRAPHY MAP

STEEP SLOPE – CONTOUR LINES ARE CLOSER TOGETHER
GRADUAL SLOPE – CONTOUR LINES ARE FUTHER APART
FLAT SLOPE – CONTOUR LINES ARE VERY FAR APART

8. Flood zones, water characteristics, and FEMA

Are you aware of any flood areas on the property? You might have heard of a hundred- or five-hundred-year flood plain; you can typically find this information in a map layer on GIS websites. This view will give you

an idea of how much flood plain is on a parcel, but you should hire a professional engineer or surveyor to determine this exact information.

Understanding FEMA flood zones.

FEMA stands for Federal Emergency Management Agency. This agency within the Department of Homeland Security coordinates the federal response to natural or manmade disasters. FEMA defines flood zones (geographical areas) according to levels of flood risk for properties located near natural water structures like creeks, lakes, and oceans. FEMA creates maps to outline a community's flood risk.

How does FEMA affect a parcel? If a parcel touches a creek, lake, or the ocean, for example, FEMA and local governments have established guidelines that tell the distance, or setback, a structure must be from this designated flood plain, flood hazard area, or flood zone. Setbacks vary for each water feature, but this is a critical piece of information to know when selling or purchasing lots or land. To understand this better, visit the FEMA website at www.fema.gov and look under "Flood Hazard Mapping."

NOTE: Flood plain areas on a parcel can also affect the insurance required by the insurance company and the lender. Flood insurance covers a structure located near a flood plain, and sometimes the cost is quite high. This is definitely a fact that should be researched prior to closing a property.[22]

9. Impervious surfaces

What are impervious surfaces? Impervious surfaces are mainly artificial structures (such as pavement, sidewalks, and driveways) that are water resistant and do not allow water to infiltrate or enter into the soil. Too much impervious surface in a particular area prevents normal rainfall from replenishing the groundwater and affects the water quality of local streams, the streamflow, and flooding characteristics. This can become a problem as cities grow and natural landscapes and vegetation are replaced with streets or roads, residential developments, sidewalks, and parking lots. When impervious surface is increased, the water runoff has to be redirected, instead of draining naturally into the soil, causing streams to overflow and potential flooding of local water sources.[23]

> **NOTE:** The amount of impervious surface on a property will have specific guidelines restricting land use and density put in place by governmental agencies. These same agencies might also require additional fees to be paid by the developer for this impervious surface.

10. Stormwater runoff

What is stormwater runoff and what are the issues? During heavy rainfall or snowstorms, the ground can become saturated or frozen. The water or melting snow that rapidly flows over saturated ground or impervious surfaces is called stormwater runoff. As cities expand, stormwater management and watershed protection agencies develop restrictions and

regulations for proper land grading and limitations on the amount of impervious surface area allowed. These regulations manage and control flow and retention of the water runoff allowing for slow absorption and minimizing potential flood conditions. This is also crucial to filtering and minimizing pollutants from entering streams, lakes, and oceans. In land development, a plan is designed and laid out during the engineering phase to control stormwater runoff and comply with the state and local standards.[24, 25]

You may be thinking to yourself right about now that this is a lot of information to learn, and you would be right. However, most of this information is discovered during a buyer's investigation period or due diligence period. You, as an agent, can be a huge asset by discovering much of this information prior to a listing or purchase simply by asking questions and doing some homework. Of course there are a lot of things in this chapter that we cannot and do not have the expertise to uncover, but as you get more comfortable with land, you will know what to look for through questions and research. Often, a lot of information is discovered in the deeds, as we will discuss in the next chapter.

"The most profitable investment on the land is land."[26]

–Amit Kalantri

4 Understanding the Deeds

Story: The expensive lesson ...

One of my business partners and I found a property owner who had four lots in a neighborhood that they were in the process of subdividing into seven lots to sell. The current zoning for the property would allow the lots to be subdivided, so they began to move forward by hiring a surveyor, paying the county fees for approvals, and spending quite a bit of time and money in the process. Soon thereafter, the owner listed the seven lots for sale, and a local builder put them under contract. During the due diligence period, the buyer's attorney found a glitch in the title. Twenty-five years prior, a deed restriction had been added to the lots in the neighborhood that stated that the lot setbacks could not be altered without a certain percentage of the

existing homeowners in the subdivision agreeing to the change. Without agreement to reduce the setbacks, the property would not accommodate seven lots.

All of the owners of the neighborhood had to be tracked down to get documents signed agreeing to this change, adding yet another cost to the owner of the now seven vacant lots. As time went by without successfully locating the property owners and acquiring the appropriate number of signatures, the builder terminated the contract. The owner of the seven lots then had two choices: continue trying to get those deed restrictions changed or spend more money reverting the seven lots back to the original four.

What did we learn from this? That it would be wise to read all deed restrictions prior to attempting changes to any property you or your clients may own.

This chapter provides an overview of how deeds work, who prepares them, the different types available, and some of the issues you might find with deeds.

1. What is a deed to a property?

Every parcel of land has a deed, which is a written legal document that allows for the transfer of property from one individual, business, or entity to another. Deeds are typically recorded at the county courthouse, and you can obtain a copy at the register of deeds office at the county courthouse and online where counties offer online service. Typically, during the due diligence phase of the contract, an attorney and/or title company will perform a title search and research the deed.[27]

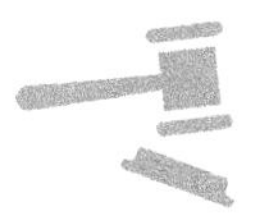

NOTE: The deed is referenced by the legal description.

2. Who has the deed, or where can you find a copy of a deed?

The property owner should have a copy of the deed, but you can also obtain a copy from the local county register of deeds office. They can search for the deed by the property owner's name, property address, or legal description. They may charge a small fee for this request.

3. Who prepares a deed?

Whatever name is on the recorded deed is the most current owner of the property and the legal seller. Often, a buyer will select an attorney to close a transaction, and the seller will pay the buyer's attorney's fee for deed preparation. However, the seller may choose to hire their own attorney to represent them, prepare the deed, and ensure that the deed is completed properly and the transfer is successful.[28]

4. What does a deed contain?

A deed is an important legal document typically prepared by an attorney or a title company. Many disputes are settled by checking the deed to a property to verify ownership. Each state has its own requirements. However, every deed must be in writing to be enforcable in a court of law and should contain the following information:

- Wording that states it is a deed and the type of deed it is.

- The property description in metes and bounds (boundary lines of the land), which might refer to a map of the property that is recorded at the register of deeds office in the county courthouse. They tend to use the government rectangular survey method in the Midwest.
- The signatures of the individual or entity transferring the property, known as the Grantor.
- Information regarding who is taking title to the property.[29]

5. What are some different types of deeds and their purposes?

General warranty deed

The general warranty deed offers the most protection to the buyer because this deed covers the property's entire history. The seller makes legal promises that they will protect the buyer against any claims or demands on the seller prior to the transferring of the property.

Deed of trust

This is an agreement between a lender and a borrower that allows a third party to serve as a trustee until the borrower pays off the debt.[30]

What is the difference between a mortgage and a deed of trust? With a deed of trust, as stated above, there are three parties involved: the borrower, the lender, and the trustee. With a mortgage document, there are two parties involved: the borrower and the lender.[31]

Quitclaim deed

A quitclaim deed, also known as a non-warranty deed, is a legal instrument used to transfer interest in real property. The owner/grantor terminates (quits) any right and claim to the property, thereby allowing the right or claim to transfer to the recipient/grantee.[32, 33]

Example: This is often used in a divorce situation when one spouse transfers all the ownership rights or interest in the marital property to the other spouse. Or, it may be used to change a business ownership name to a different entity name.

Warranty deed

In a warranty deed, the grantor (seller) guarantees that he or she holds clear title to a piece of real estate and has a right to sell it to the grantee (buyer). This is in contrast to a quitclaim deed, where the seller offers no guarantees as to ownership.[34]

Example: This is typically used in a real estate transaction between a buyer and seller.

Correction deed

A correction deed serves to correct and negate a mistake made between parties that have contracted an original deed agreement. The mistake can cover minor terms of the agreement (such as the misspelling of a name) or major terms (such as the price or amount of acreage of the land).[35]

Example: My last name is Sain, but if my name were accidentally misspelled Saine in a deed, then that must be corrected.

Transfer on death deed

A transfer on death (TOD) deed, or sometimes referred to as a beneficiary deed, is a special type of deed that can be used to transfer ownership of real estate outside probate in a growing number of US states. You will need to check with an attorney to understand the specifics of this deed and if this deed is appropriate for your particular situation.[36]

Example: A parent may prepare this type of deed so that upon his or her death, the property goes to a child.

Special warranty deed or limited warranty deed

Investopedia defines a special warranty deed or limited warranty deed as a case where the seller of the property warrants only against anything that occurred during the seller's physical ownership. In other words, the grantor doesn't guarantee against any defects in clear title that existed before the grantor took possession of the property.[37]

> **NOTE:** We typically see these types of deeds with a foreclosure property where the bank owned the property for a short amount of time but does not guarantee there was a clear title prior to foreclosing on the property.

Example: It's sad but true that deeds can really complicate these sales. Ever hear of a property being sold twice, at the same time, and the second sale's deed was recorded before the first sale was recorded? Guess who owns the property! Yep, you guessed it, the one who got the deed recorded first, even though

the sale happened after the first sale. This has happened all too often lately, and there have even been cases of fraud with deed recordation. Meaning, people are shocked to discover they no longer own the real estate they thought was theirs. That is why the laws and rules for selling, recording, and releasing funds are now so strict. First, the attorney must establish proof of who the actual parties are on both sides of the sale. The deed is not (or should not be) recorded until after the sale to ensure the right person gets the property and all leins cleared. Finally, the funds are released to the seller after proof that the deed recordation has been completed. This has been my personal experience in the past. These rules protect the innocent, honest people in today's real estate market. In North Carolina we refer to this as a pure notice or "pure race" state, as in "first one to record wins." To my knowledge, not every state is a pure notice state.

> **NOTE:** Check your particular state's rules for recording deeds to make certain you and your clients are protected properly.

To further research the three types of recording statutes on your own (Notice Acts, Race Acts, and Race-Notice Acts) check out an article in *Property Law for Dummies by Alan R. Romero: https://www.dummies.com/education/law/distinguishing-the-three-types-of-recording-statutes/.*

You may have figured out by now that you will want to read through the deed of your client's

potential purchase or sale. Although most of us are not attorneys, we may be able to catch something in a deed prior to a listing or closing that throws up a red flag; then we can do the research necessary to prevent delays and bring it to the attention of the client. It could be something as simple as a noted easement that the owner either did not know or forgot about. So, start to familiarize yourself with deed verbiage. Not to give legal advice—because we are not attorneys, so leave that to the professionals—but just to become more knowledgeable and a better asset to your clients.

By now you may be overwhelmed at all of the things a broker has to do to ensure a successful transaction. That's the point of this book! Our job description as agents may not be what you originally thought. I tell people my job is to help others get to a transparent, successful closing. That often means going far above the normal duties required to ensure my clients are protected.

"I've learned that people will forget what you said, people will forget what you did, but people will never forget how you made them feel."[38]

–Carl W. Buehner

“If you are lucky, you will have the opportunity in your life to be owned by a good piece of land.”[39]

–Daniel J. Rice

5

Surveys and Why They Are Important

Story: The altered survey … whodunit?

This is a good story about the importance of surveys.

When I was a rookie agent, I listed a vacant lot for an owner (Jill). I found a buyer who was a custom homebuilder (Mike). I shared with Mike the survey Jill had given me. Jill had received the survey directly from the previous owner (Ken). Please note: I was not involved in the original purchase between Jill and Ken.

Both Jill and Mike were acquaintances of mine. I had worked previously with Mike on lot purchases, and Jill was my daughter's babysitter at the time.

During Mike's due diligence and inspection period, he discovered that the survey Jill provided had been altered. When Mike went to the courthouse to research

the lot, he found the original recorded survey showed a debris burial pit in the middle of the lot. Someone had deleted the wording "debris burial pit" from the survey Ken provided to the current owner, Jill.

Jill had no idea she had purchased a lot that contained a debris burial pit. She had trusted Ken and decided to save some money by not paying to have another survey performed on the lot she was purchasing from Ken at that time. Had she paid for a current survey prior to closing, she would have discovered this discrepancy, and my guess is she would not have purchased the lot from Ken.

Mike had to hire a company to complete soil borings and soil testing to discover exactly where the pit was located. It was an expensive task, but in the end, Mike was able to find enough good soil on the lot to build a house. Jill literally went to the site every day to pray over the findings on the soils as the borings were being drilled. Prayer works, I'm just saying! However, Jill did have to offer a discount on the purchase price to offset the cost of the extensive testing.

Mystery of whodunit? Unsolved!

NOTE: If I had been working with Jill when she bought the property from Ken, I would have advised her to get a new or updated survey. A survey can uncover hidden issues prior to closing or even stop a closing. Get a survey! It's great insurance to know what you are buying or selling.

Surveys are crucial to have at the time of purchase. If a buyer relies on the previous survey instead of having one done when they buy the property, then later some sort of issue arises between property owners as to encroachments or easements, the buyer's title insurance policy will NOT cover that discrepancy. Brokers, go on record that you advised your clients to have their own survey done prior to closing. If they refuse to spend the money, have them sign something stating that you advised them of this. Moving the corner of a fence might not cost too much to make right. But moving the corner of a three-car, brick detached garage is a whole other story. Don't you be the one to pay for that mistake!

Also, no matter how comfortable you may be with reading a survey, do NOT interpret it for your client. If they ask about an item on the survey, refer them to the surveyor or attorney to explain. Unless you are a licensed surveyor, don't act like one.

Surveys today are much more accurate than in the past. Surveying is a highly technical and complex service using the art of measuring, mathematics, and proper interpretation of real property law. It might cost more than you might expect, but in the end, the investment can save you money and headaches. It is an inexpensive insurance policy for the buyer to know exactly what they are getting.

In the business of land, each parcel of land has boundaries or lot/property dimensions that describe the shape and number of acres within the boundaries. These lot dimensions are the information that a

surveyor is verifying about a tract of land. Many times during my career, a landowner did not actually own what they thought they did. Sometimes they owned more; sometimes they owned less. This information was discovered through surveying. Additionally, a survey includes whether any physical features overlap with the adjacent properties. This might reveal encroachments that in some way may adversely affect the title to the land.[40]

When I first wrote this chapter, I wanted to keep it short and sweet. However, as I began to research the topic and its importance, the chapter kept growing because its significance became clearer to me. I highly encourage you to pay close attention as this chapter covers how vital it is to every piece of property to have a current and accurate survey and to understand what type of survey you might need. Even if the seller's survey is current, I prefer having a licensed surveyor perform a new survey. If you continue growing in your real estate career, you will run across one of the surveys discussed in this chapter at some point.

For additional information to include in this chapter, I contacted the North Carolina Surveyors Society president, Tim Bowes. I hope the following section will help provide you with a better understanding of surveying and its importance (thanks, Tim!), but you can always contact a local surveyor in your area to inquire about the type of survey needed for your particular situation.

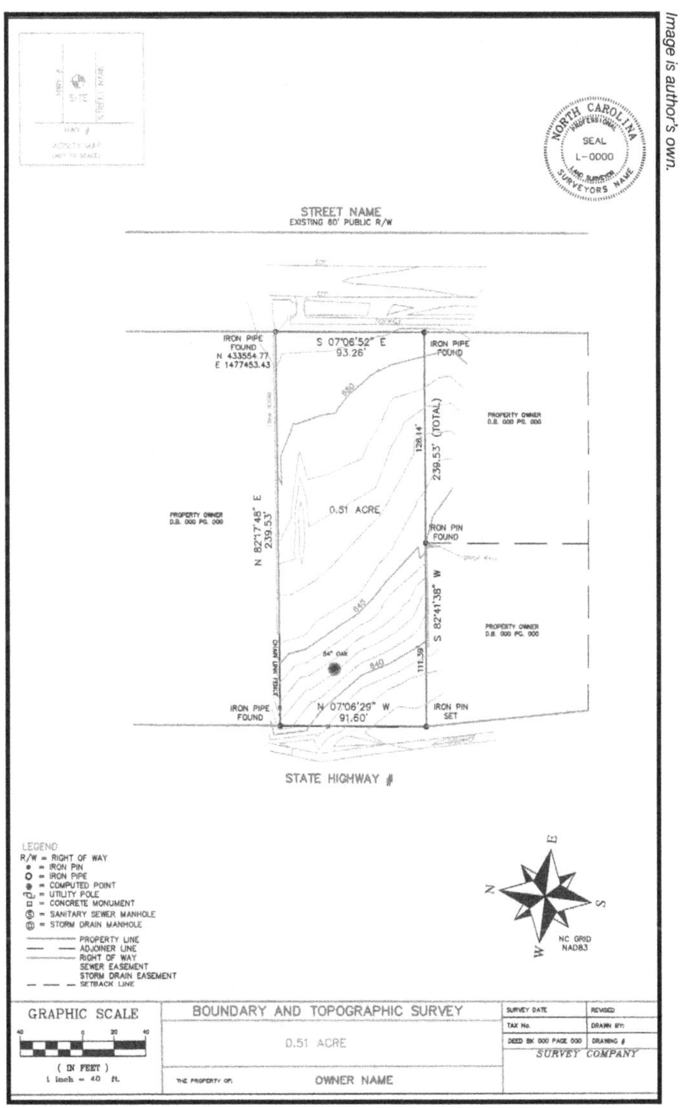

Image is author's own.

Above is a sample of a survey.

1. What is a survey?

A survey is a process used to identify a property's corners, points, or pins and measure the distances between them. These points are used to create boundaries for ownership and land maps. Depending on the type of survey you or your client orders, residential or commercial, it can show roads, structures, utility easements, creeks, fences, encroachments, and many other things that you might not initially see on the property.

2. What are the different types of surveys and their characteristics?

Because many types of surveys exist, only the most common types and their uses are listed below.

Plat map

Often referred to as a plat, this kind of survey will show how a track of land is divided into lots. It shows the size, boundary locations, streets, flood zones, and easements. This is what residential agents see more than any other surveys. These plat maps are drawn up by civil engineers when creating the development and approved by the county planning department.

What is the difference between a plat and a plot? These two words sound similar but are very different. A plat is a map of land, such as a neighborhood as described above, and a plot is a piece of land, like a lot used for a single purpose such as a house or a park. within the plat map.[41]

Boundary survey

This type of survey is used to mark a property's boundary lines. The surveyor will research the deed and public records to begin the process. They will then mark the parcel corners with monuments, irons, pipes, concrete markers, nails, and the like. The surveyor identifies the parcel lines and produces a detailed map or plat to show the results of the survey.

Topographic survey

This type of survey shows the measurements of elevation points on a parcel of land and charts the elevations using contour lines on a map.

As-built survey or record survey

These surveys are often prepared at the end of construction to meet a lender's or municipality's requirements. These surveys provide a record of how a project was constructed according to approved construction drawings. This survey usually reflects all building, curb, parking lot features, utilities, sanitary sewer, storm drainage facilities, and other structures. They are mainly used to evaluate completion of projects, issuance of final permits, or final payments to contractors.

Physical/mortgage/loan survey

This type of survey is primarily used in the purchase of a single-family home. The survey shows the property boundaries, location of the home with dimension and distance to property lines, improvements on

the property (outbuildings, walkways, patios, decks, pools, ponds, significant landscape features, driveways, impervious areas, etc.). Since title insurance companies began to insure the loan policies without exception for "matters of survey," the lenders have no need to require this. Just because it is not an exception or requirement on the loan policies, does not mean it is not still an exception or requirement on the owner's insurance policies. I always recommend a current survey just to be safe in all areas.

Foundation survey

This survey measures the position of a foundation that has been built or poured on a parcel. It provides dimensions from the corners of the foundation to the nearest property line and can show elevations of foundation walls or footings. This survey is used to ensure that the foundation was built in the approved location of the plot plan, site plan, or construction drawing.

Subdivision survey

This survey is a boundary survey that divides a parcel into two or more smaller properties, like a lot. A plat is created by the surveyor in accordance with the governing authority's development ordinance, which regulates land subdivisions, and is then recorded in the register of deeds/registrar's/land records office.

Existing conditions/engineering/design survey

This type of survey incorporates a topography survey, as-built survey, and, possibly, a boundary survey, which results in a plot of the survey measurements in the form of drawings and observations for specified engineering design.

Construction survey

This survey involves the surveyor making calculations and measurements to stake out points by marking them on the ground. These guidelines for the points or markings come from the approved construction plan. This is to guide the contractors and construction of the structures or roads to be built.[42, 43]

ALTA/NSPS land title survey

This type of survey is used mainly in commercial property and for sales of large tracts of land but is not limited to those areas. The American Land Title Association (ALTA) and National Society of Professional Surveyors (NSPS) jointly developed and adopted these survey and mapping standards to assure the title industry's needs were met and addressed at a reasonable cost and in an acceptable time frame by the survey process.

To my knowledge, no bank in the United States will lend money to develop or purchase real property without obtaining a title insurance policy. A title policy will list survey exceptions, and the only way to qualify or remove them is to have a land title survey performed. This survey discloses potential title

problems and can provide a measure of assurance that one's investment is not a risk. This survey involves extensive research into public and private records by the surveyor and title attorney. It also requires extensive analysis after collecting field evidence and comparing it to the recorded documents.

After analysis and fieldwork are completed, a plat/map is prepared, and a standardized survey certification is placed on the plat/map. Each state's survey laws and regulations are followed and used, unless there is a conflict with the ALTA/ NSPS standards, to ensure the licensed surveying professional can issue his/her seal and certification.

An ALTA survey can find hidden easements or right-of-ways. Some developers may have to tear down buildings, or projects may be delayed to go back for plan changes and approvals through the municipalities because they did not get an ALTA survey prior to construction. It is better to be safe than sorry.

Depending on the size and location of the property, the complexity of or problems with the legal description, the number and clarity of easements, and the amount of improvements and utilities on the property, the fee for a land title survey can run from perhaps $2,000 at the very low end to several hundred thousand dollars at the high end. The effort could take anywhere from a week to several months.[44]

3. Who can legally prepare a survey?

The practice of land surveying is subject to regulations to safeguard life, health, and property and to

promote the public welfare. A survey is prepared by a professional licensed surveyor (PLS) in accordance with each state's general statutes and rules.

4. Who pays for the survey?

Most of the time, the buyer of real property pays for the survey. As it is a transaction between two parties, the cost of the survey can be negotiated between the buyer and seller.

The professional land surveyor's fee will include the time to search for deeds or court records, to locate the physical boundary evidence at the property, to make the necessary computations to check the boundary, to place appropriate markers on the property, and to prepare the survey map.

The cost of the survey will vary because of missing corner evidence, disputed boundary lines, rough terrain, heavy underbrush, poor land descriptions, and travel time to and from the property. These variables make it difficult for the professional land surveyor to predict an exact cost or when your survey will be completed. Depending on the professional land surveyor's schedule and difficulty of work, the cost and completion schedule might need to be negotiated with the surveyor.

5. Who owns the survey?

The survey plat and report are owned by the person or entity who contracts with the surveyor. The owner of the survey should not attempt to sell, distribute, or manipulate the plat, map, report, design plan,

subdivision plan, opinions, plat notes, certificates, or any other similar document without the consent of the surveyor, unless negotiated differently in the contract. The surveyor remains in control of all field data, CAD files, field books, and related material, as well as any copyright materials associated with the surveyor.

6. Are surveys recorded and available as a public record?

Surveys can be recorded as a public record. Most governing municipalities and counties have notes and certificates they require to be placed on a survey map in order to have it recorded. If the survey is to be recorded, the person or entity ordering the survey should notify the surveyor of the intent to record when the survey is contracted. This early request will prevent additional costs or services for making a survey recordable after it is complete. The surveyor can then prepare the survey in accordance with the governing rules and laws for recordable documents.

7. Can previous surveys be copied in marketing materials in the sale of the property?

Previous surveys or any part of surveys should not be copied in marketing materials for the future sale of the property without the consent of the licensed professional land surveyor who signed and sealed the survey. Otherwise, contact the state licensing board that administers the rules and laws under which surveyors practice. However, the owner of the survey could allow the use in marketing materials.

8. Are surveys copyrighted?

It depends. Some surveys or material produced by the surveyor are protected under copyright laws. The absence of a copyright symbol on a document does not mean it is not copyrighted. Perhaps the surveyor or business entity has not registered the copyright. Should there be any question about the copyright for the survey, contact the surveyor, the state licensing board, or a copyright attorney to avoid any potential violations.

9. Who reads and interprets surveys?

Many professionals, public and private agencies, and lay people read and interpret surveys. Engineers, architects, contractors, real estate professionals, tax assessors, attorneys, homeowners, FEMA employees, GIS professionals, and other surveyors read and review many kinds of surveys. However, as a real estate broker, I would suggest to NEVER interpret a survey for your client. If they have a question, refer them to the surveyor.

10. Are surveys dated to show the property as of a specific date?

Surveys that are signed and sealed by a licensed professional surveyor bearing the date they signed and sealed the survey will contain a certification that states the date(s) the survey was performed. The survey represents the moment in time in which it was performed.

11. Are surveyors required to mark the boundaries and corners of the property with wooden stakes and colored ribbons?

In most states, surveyors are required to monument (mark) property corners that have been lost or removed when a boundary survey is performed. Monuments must be of a permanent nature such as a concrete monument, a metal stake, or a PK nail concrete nail in asphalt. A PK nail is a thick nail with an indentation in the middle of its head.

Where a corner falls in a right-of-way, tree, stream, fence post, boulder, stone, or similar object, one or more monuments or metal stakes shall be placed in the boundary so that the inaccessible point may be located accurately on the ground and the map.

The wooden stakes generally are set near the property corner as a witness to mark the property corner found or set. Other witness posts used are white PVC pipes, metal fence posts, wooden fence posts, small cut trees (pickets), and, in cases of municipal/government boundaries, three-foot-tall Carsonite posts with an identifying label for that property corner.

The predominant ribbon color used today to mark found or set property corners and property lines is bright pink. Some surveyors use bright orange, as that was the predominant marking color for survey boundaries and stakes until the past decade.

12. What is the purpose and definition of metal pins?

The metal pin used in surveying is a two- to three-foot-long rod or rebar with a specific identification number to mark the property corner with a material of a permanent nature. This marking pin satisfies the rules and laws for surveying procedures in many states. A metal pin also makes locating a corner easier in the future when searching for it with a metal detector.

13. Are surveys required to show flood plains, flood lines, and flood zones?

Depending on the type of survey requested, a boundary survey is not required to show flood plains, flood lines, or flood areas unless crossing or forming a boundary line of the property shown.

14. Are surveys required to state the acreage and dimensions of the property?

In many states, surveys are required to state the acreage and show dimensions of property surveyed. Distances are recorded in feet or meters and decimals.

15. What is the purpose of the surveyor's seal on the survey?

The surveyor's seal and signature on the survey ensure the survey and plat were performed by or performed under the direct supervision of a licensed, professional land surveyor to the standards of practice for land surveying for the state where the surveyor is legally registered to practice. It also means the licensed

professional surveyor has reviewed and approved the survey/plat/report to be sent out as a final work product.

16. What if a buyer decides not to order a survey?

When a buyer decides not to order a survey, it is like purchasing a house without a home inspection or a used car without taking it to a mechanic. If a survey is not ordered, a seller will offer a general warranty deed that transfers all rights and interests they have and a buyer will be asked to sign an affidavit stating they accept the property as-is/where-is. In this case, the title company will exclude any matters a current survey of the property may have shown. Basically, the title company is limiting their liability to what is known and will place on the buyer the burden and cost of any matters that show up after the purchase.

The following URL is for a surveyor brochure from the North Carolina Society of Surveyors at ncsurveyors.com: (http://ncsurveyors.com/files/PDFs/Protecting%20Your%20Biggest%20Investment%20-%20Watermark.pdf).[45]

If your state offers a similar guide, it is good to offer it to clients or occasionally review it as a refresher.

> **NOTE:** Again, I suggest you review the rules, requirements, and regulations pertaining to your particular state regarding surveys.

17. What are the most common issues for surveyors?

The most common issue for surveyors is the frequency of calls from disgruntled homeowners of newly

purchased homes who want to build a fence, shed, deck expansion, or something similar. Their complaint is that their contractor is unable to obtain a permit from the county to start the project because the homebuilder only provided a foundation survey for the development not a closing survey. Homeowners assume the survey they have in hand at closing is sufficient for future exterior home modifications and improvements. To save homeowners time, money, and frustration, agents should urge them to order closing or boundary surveys at completion of construction and prior to closing.

Setbacks could be another concern. Setbacks are the distance from the property line or boundary to be maintained between structures. These setbacks are normally decided by the local government.

18. What are the most common issues for boundary surveys?

Surveyors have shared instances where they have surveyed parcels of land with a creek as a boundary line, and a buyer and a seller had agreed to a purchase price based on the acreage in the deed or plat. The seller's survey plat was thirty to fifty years old, but since the last surveys were taken, hurricanes, floods, and other natural occurrences could have changed the nature of the property boundary.[46]

Example: Severe rainfall events cause creeks to overflow their banks and cut new channels (or a new path for the water to flow). Property lines move to follow the new creek causing changes in

the property boundary and, more importantly, the property acreage. A seller might have lost acres of land because of natural occurrences. Therefore, the buyer wants a price reduction. Had the buyer not requested a new survey, the inaccurate assumption would have provided less land than offered for purchase. On the other hand, the seller may have gained acreage with the new path of water flow.

Understanding that there are different types of surveys and the need for your specific situations cannot be expressed enough, in my opinion. A survey is one of the most important things to acquire during a purchase. Even if you are a seller and may have inherited the property, get a survey so that you will know and understand exactly what you have. You may be surprised to learn that you have more or less property than you originally thought. There may be easements on the property that you are unaware of. A survey will give you more information on a property than you can find on your own. An accurate, current survey will allow you to discover your options in the zoning of a project, which will be the topic of the next chapter.

"If you focus on results, you will never change. If you focus on change, you will get results."[47]

–Jack Dixon

"If you fail to plan, you are planning to fail!"[48]

–Reverend H.K. Williams

Land Zoning and Density

Story: What's it worth?

Jim owned a twelve-acre piece of property with a rental house that he purchased as farmland years ago. His goal was to hold onto the property and wait for the value to increase as the town grew. After he had owned the property for many years, a group of investors approached him with an offer to purchase the property at considerably more than he had paid when he purchased it. Being careful not to respond too quickly despite the buyers inquiring several times, he decided to do a little investigating of his own. He checked the local town's future land use maps. As it turned out, his little tract of land was projected to become future zoning for a multifamily/commercial site that the town favored because of its location, and the property was worth twice what the investors offered.

Many landowners are not as knowledgeable on zoning and density as they need to be, especially if they inherited property from family members, or maybe purchased a lot or land in foreclosure. Help your clients and do some homework for them. It could be to everyone's financial advantage.

To better understand zoning, you need to be aware that every piece of property has a zoning designation assigned by the county where the property is located. Even the smallest parcel of land has a zoning designation. This important information determines whether it will work for you or your client's purposes. If not, you want to know if the zoning can be changed to satisfy your needs or accommodate your plans for the property.

1. What is zoning?

Zoning is the method used by governments to control the physical development of land particularly to maintain balance of use and projected growth. Zoning laws typically specify the division of areas in which residential, industrial, recreational, or commercial activities may be developed. A parcel is assigned a zoning designation by the county, city, or town to control and direct the development of the property. Zoning effectively establishes for what and how the property can currently be used.[49]

2. How do you find the zoning designation and its requirements?

To find a particular property's zoning, you can call the planning department or, quite often, find

it on the GIS website. You will need to know the property address, parcel ID number, or owner's name to make the inquiry. You can find what a particular zoning designation requires by going to the appropriate governing body's website and reviewing the ordinances.

For example, a county nearby has one type of zoning called R-40, which means one house can stand per 40,000 sq. ft. of land, or about one house per acre. If you are a city dweller, that might seem like a lot of land for only one house, but if you live in the country or a rural area, it might seem small. A C-1 designation might be commercial or industrial zoning. Each county has its own zoning guidelines, and they are all different. It is important to understand zoning for the county or municipality in which you are selling or buying land.

3. What is a rezoning?

A zoning classification is not necessarily permanent. Zoning designations often can be changed, or conditional zonings approved, depending on the situation. This is accomplished through a process called rezoning. This change is sought when the current zoning of a property will not work for a potential buyer's or owner's intended use. Potential zoning maps or future land use maps may assist a property owner in obtaining a more profitable zoning.

What are future land use maps? This is a community's guide for future planning. Depending on your state and how it is divided up, municipalities

or townships will work diligently to hire outside resources to study and lay out plans on maps for what they envision for the future growth of the municipality or township. This usually takes into consideration economic development, transportation, housing, and other necessary concerns.

To see what your local land use plan looks like, contact your municipality or go to the website and look it up. It will typically be a colored map with areas showing where certain types of construction or development would be favorable to the municipality or township. There is a legend that is color-coded for certain densities in certain areas or for where they want to keep more open or green space. This is a great tool for agents to understand what a town wants to see in the future for development. This can help you to educate your client as to what possibly could be developed on a potential property.

The property owner or buyer submits an application for a request to rezone through the county, city, or town's zoning department. Whether rezoning is approved or not is up to the elected officials. They typically remain consistent with adopted plans for the area and follow recommendations from their planning board. Approved rezoning allows the buyer or current owner to have the desired zoning for the property.

Rezoning a property can be a relatively short process if there is no resistance from surrounding property owners and if the rezoning is beneficial for the long-term plans for the municipality. If the rezoning is not in alignment with projected

development, it could be a much longer process. Ultimately, the time frame depends on the county and/or local municipalities and their particular requirements to rezone. To learn about your area, consult with an engineer for the municipality or county, or with an attorney who is knowledgeable about the process in that particular county.

To get more information, call your county, city, or town's zoning department. Be prepared to provide either the parcel ID number or address so the staff can look up the zoning for the property you are researching. Alternatively, you can go to the GIS website for the county where the property is located.

> **NOTE:** To use the GIS website to locate the zoning for the parcel, go to the Labels tab and click "Zoning." You may have to zoom in on the map for the zoning designation to appear. By no means is this information guaranteed to be accurate. You should always call the zoning department for the county, city, or town and ask them to confirm the zoning for a particular parcel of land.

4. What is the density of a property?

Density is the number of units or lots that the county or municipality will allow per acre of land.

5. Where can you find permitted density information?

You will have to look up the zoning requirements for your county to know what the zoning designations mean, or you can call the planning and zoning department to find the permitted density for a property as well as future potential zoning. Future

potential zoning is typically based on adopted comprehensive plans, land use plans, and/or small area plans for the property.

The planning and zoning department can also tell you about setbacks for buildings, wetland issues, FEMA policies, endangered species, storm water controls, tree ordinances, transportation, future land use plans, and many other considerations required by the county.

Much of the information above will ultimately become the responsibility of the buyer during the due diligence or inspection period. As an agent, however, you should know how and where to get this information. Whether you are looking for a property for a specific client or listing a property, you should be able to locate zoning and density information.

6. What is the importance of zoning and density for any property?

A residential zoning typically means single-family housing. Commercial zoning is typically associated with businesses—such as warehouses, apartment complexes, and retail spaces. The current zoning and future potential zoning of a property determine the value and use of the property. For example, if a residential zoning is changed to a commercial zoning, it could drastically increase the value of the property. Likewise, property value might be adversely affected by an undesirable zoning nearby, such as a landfill.

Zoning determines property density. Density is measured in dwellings per acre. A residential zoning

with a density of one or two houses per acre could potentially be rezoned for multi-family use, changing its density. This would allow more housing units per acre, increasing the property value. Researching zoning and density of the surrounding properties is just as important as knowing the zoning and density of the property you are considering.

Let's say you or your client are purchasing a home in a neighborhood that backs up to a beautiful wooded area or creek. What is the current and potential zoning for the land adjacent (across the creek) to that property? Is it residential or potentially commercial? Will more houses, a multi-family site, or, even worse, a factory be built there? The view and privacy that attracted you or your clients to the property could be diminished or disappear completely with a rezoning.

Story: The unforeseen timbering hurricane

Such a thing happened to me. In 2019 I purchased my brother's house, which was on a one-acre parcel of land next door to my folks who own a small eight-acre farm. On the other side of my house was a beautiful forest of twenty-five acres that had always been there, creating a very secluded, private setting for my newly acquired home. The home was set way back in the woods on a long gravel driveway and you could not see it from the road. This home was completely surrounded by trees except for the high tension powerline path on the back side, which allowed for

extra parking and a place for my kids to hang out, not to mention the deer that came through on a daily basis. About a year after I had purchased the property, I noticed what I thought was a driveway being cut into the property next door (the twenty-five acres of forest). I thought to myself, Hey, I am getting a new neighbor. So, I stopped by to speak to the gentleman on the bulldozer to inquire as to what was coming next door. Much to my surprise, I found out they were about to timber the entire twenty-five acres, leaving my little, private country setting exposed to the rest of the world. Turns out the twenty-five-acre track made an L shape around my little, private setting, and after the logging company was through, it looked like I was in the middle of a field.

I knew the owners of the land, and they were absentee owners. They lived in another state and just wanted the money for the timber. How do I know this? I called them, of course. They did not have to look at the property on a daily basis; in my experience it probably did not matter to them what it looked like. To add insult to injury, the logging company did not chip the scrap wood, and it looked like a hurricane had come through after they had completed the job and just left a mess, as hurricanes do. Now, that is what I look at every day when I am home. So, my point to this story is to make your clients aware of the possibilities of the potential for a changing environment when they are purchasing properties that butt up against someone else's. One day the scenery may change, and they need to be prepared for that possibility.

On a separate note, if you find yourself in a similar situation like I did, the best thing to do is to be nice to the loggers and see if they can possibly leave you a treed buffer. Remember as well, the loggers are just getting paid to do a job they were hired for, so don't get mad at them for something they cannot control. These guys have interesting stories to tell about adjacent landowners and the threats they make toward them. If you are nice to them, they may leave you a few trees for a buffer that normally they would have taken. These guys work harder than I ever want to. I witnessed this for three weeks straight. Being nice goes a long way in today's society, as it is becoming a rarity; I promise they won't forget you, and you may get to keep an extra tree or two.

> **NOTE:** Adjacent property could possibly be rezoned, so knowing the future potential zoning or (the future land use plan) is important.

7. What is the difference between zoning and deed restrictions?

Zoning ordinances are regulations that are political and mandatory and recorded as local laws. Deed restrictions are voluntary, contractual agreements between private parties recorded in private deeds to spell out specific limitations of use. These can be restrictions on a single property between private parties or neighborhood covenants. Because covenants are voluntary and typically neighborhood specific, they may be more restrictive than zoning ordinances.[50]

8. Who enforces zoning and deed restrictions?

Local government officials enforce county or town zonings and deed restrictions. For personal property, the owner who initiated the deed restriction on the property will likely enforce it. In a neighborhood, a homeowners association comprised of elected homeowners enforces deed restrictions and neighborhood covenants.[51]

> **NOTE:** Zoning ordinances are public land use controls. Deed restrictions are private land use controls.

Just remember:

- The state has laws.
- The county has laws and regulations.
- The city has laws and regulations.
- The HOA has restrictions and covenants.
- Each of these entities has laws and/or regulations to be followed.

9. Who is responsible for researching deed restrictions?

Deeds and their restrictions can be interpreted differently depending on who is reading them. Anyone can research a deed. However, to be on the safe side and avoid liability, I highly suggest hiring an attorney to research a deed's restrictions. No matter where you are considering purchasing property, confirm that zoning or deed restrictions concur with the desired uses for the property.[52]

It is important to understand the zoning, future planning, and current restrictions regarding property in and around your clients' interested property. A simple explanation of what zoning is and the potential for a zoning change for a property in the future can help you and your client make an educated decision whether to move forward with a purchase or sale. Is now the right time to buy or sell? Alternatively, should you wait for future growth to capture a bigger pay day? Is the property in the path of growth and in the current overlay plan for a higher use than currently zoned? These are questions that you will want to consider for yourself or your clients. And once you have found your property, you will want to see what the soils will allow you to do on the property, so let's take a look at that in the next chapter.

"Discovery consists of looking at the same thing as everyone else and thinking something different."[53]

–Albert Szent-Györgyi

Soil Testing: How and Why

Story: Who's got gas?

Bob, a real estate broker, had a friend named Pete who owned some vacant land. Though the property was not listed for sale, Pete had been repeatedly contacted by an interested buyer named Joe. Due to Joe's persistence, Pete asked Bob the broker to research the value of the property.

Bob was curious about Joe's interest in the property, so he did a little research on Joe as well. He discovered that Joe happened to work for a natural gas company. This intrigued Bob, so he asked Pete if he would be interested in hiring a contractor to perform some borings on the property soils. Pete agreed. Through the soil borings, they discovered the land had veins of natural gas, therefore drastically increasing the previous assumed value.

Pete kept the land and sold the gas rights to the gas company for a handsome annual sum. So, what did we learn from the story? Pete's got gas, and you should know your property—particularly what is in the soil—to understand its value.

1. Why do you need to test the soil?

All dirt is not created equal. Wait, isn't dirt just dirt? Well, not exactly, and that is why we must conduct soil testing on land. Interesting fact: There are more than three hundred different types of soil in North Carolina. I had no idea.

Not only are soils tested for porosity for septic systems, they are also tested for structural capabilities in reference to foundations for houses or structures and a slew of other things. The intended use of the land will determine the type of soil testing needed.

2. How is soil testing done?

To have testing performed will depend on your intended use. Will the use be for farming, residential, a storage facility, or something else? For the sake of this book and chapter we are focused on septic systems for better understanding in the residential real estate community. To have soil testing for a septic system, you or your client will need to hire a licensed soil scientist, a geotechnical engineer firm, or use the county environmental department. They will assist in determining the soil's suitability to accept different types of septic systems based on the soil's ability to percolate (or drain, often abbreviated as "perc").

Every site is unique, and the type of testing needed will be determined by the county or soil scientist. Each county should have employees to do this. Fees vary from county to county and state to state. Remember that this usually takes a few weeks, so make sure you allow time when drawing up a purchase contract.

In some cases the local government or private consultants (soil scientists) may require large pits (three feet wide, five feet long, and up to five feet deep) excavated by a small track hoe so the county employee or soil scientist can get into the pits to examine the soil better in its natural, undisturbed state. Depending on the soil type, some soil samples may be sent to a lab for testing, then the results are given to the county to determine whether the soil is suitable for the client's desired use. The report will state the types of soil on that site and how many bedrooms will be allowed in the structure to be built as well as a diagram of where the septic lines need to be laid out.

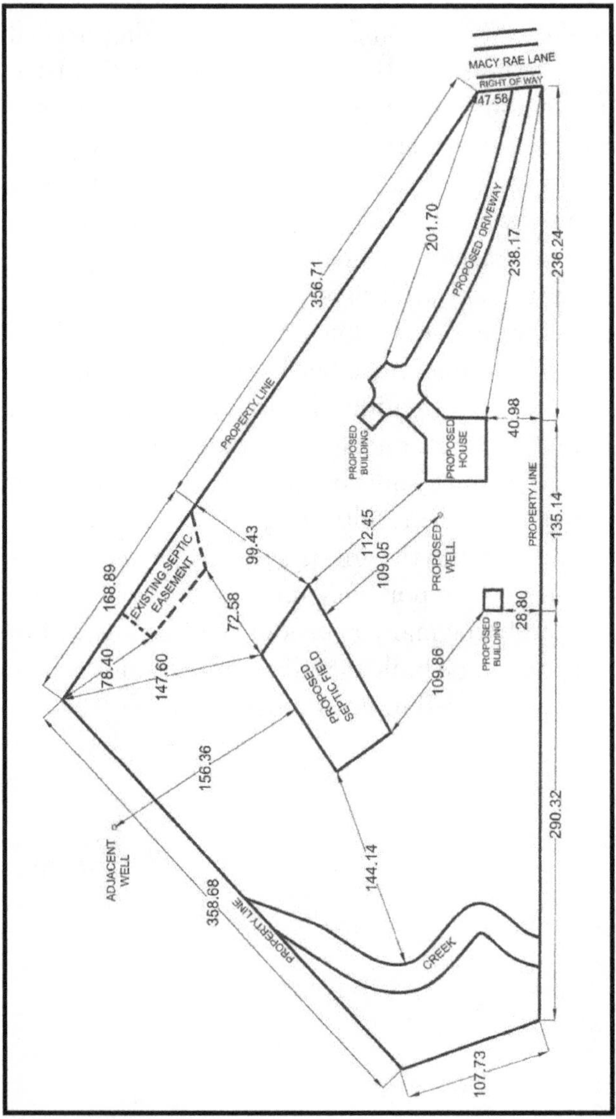

Image is author's own.

Sample of septic field tank and well.

3. What can be discovered when testing the soil?

The soil scientist looks for some of the following (but is not limited to):

- soil texture (percentages of sand, silt, or clay)
- soil structure (how particles of soil are grouped together into aggregates)
- soil consistency (strength in which the soils are held together)
- soil depth to unsuitable characteristics such as rock, the water table, etc.
- enough area for the septic system and drain fields for an initial site and sometimes a repair area backup for each site
- soil absorption ability or loading rate, which is how much the soil will absorb the effluent (liquid wastewater) into the ground

4. What is a perc (percolation) test?

What the heck is a percolation or soil suitability test? These terms are basically one and the same. These results help to determine the soil's ability to accept effluent (wastewater) over a period of time. This can be used to determine the soil's acceptable loading rate (gallons per day per square foot, or GPD/SF) and what type of septic system is needed to meet the client's needs for government approval.[54]

Why do I need a perc test?

Just remember if the property is not served by a public sewer system, the test is performed to make sure a

septic system can be installed and function properly without contaminating the drinking-water supply.

Why does the septic system determine the number of bedrooms instead of bathrooms?

If your client wants to build a home where there is no public sewer available to the property, they will definitely need to test the soil for its septic absorption capabilities. Typically, a septic system capacity and design per resident is calculated based on two persons per bedroom, which is usually sixty gallons per person for a total of 120 gallons per bedroom. The soil testing will determine how many bedrooms per resident the county will approve for that property based on the soil characteristics and the types of septic systems proposed. You will need to check your local agency to see what type of waste flow is required for each bedroom, for it may vary from state to state. The county will explain the procedure that they require for moving forward with a septic system approval application. We will go deeper into soil testing and perc tests in the next chapter.

5. Is there such a thing as bad soil?

You bet there is. The quality of the soils can be determined by hiring a local government agency or hiring a private consultant (a licensed soil scientist) to test the soils. Examples of bad soils are bull tallow or blackjack soil (expansive clay). In my experience, when wet, these soils are similar to expansive clay or playdough, but they reach the hardness of concrete

when dry and create large cracks in the soil. Either of these two conditions are unsuitable for any septic systems. Expansive clay when wet or dry will not allow for wastewater (effluent) to move downward through the soil for proper treatment, and when expansive clay is dry or hard, it will usually create large cracks in the soil and not filter the water properly before it enters the groundwater.

Another term you may hear occasionally is brownfield dirt, which is soil contamination from hazardous waste. However, soil discoveries do not mean the property is unusable. If the soils are bad in one area of the property, a structure might be better constructed elsewhere on the property. Fun fact: Ever hear of pluff mud or plough mud?[55] Well this is also a bad soil to build on. You definitely need driven piles—which are foundation supports for structures—if you want to build on pluff mud. I am obviously from the Carolinas, born and raised, so we know exactly what pluff mud is. The aroma alone gets me excited to know I am at the coast when I smell it.

So, what is pluff mud? It is the muddy salt-marsh floor. If you have ever gone oystering on the South Carolina coast, you will know what it is like to get your boot sucked off of your foot when trying to walk in this mud. Pluff mud is created by the decomposition of the plants and sea life that die in the marsh. This decomposition is what causes the aroma. Very little is known about the composition of pluff mud and its potential for practical uses in engineering. Researchers at the Citadel are continuing

to investigate the geotechnical properties of this soil as well as examining ways to improve its strength and settlement. According to Dr. Simon Ghanat, a professor at the Citadel, pluff mud is mostly made up of sand, silt, and clay. (However, to me, the trouble and total messiness is so worth the effort of oystering when you get to finally taste those delicious steamed oysters dipped in warm garlic butter. Yum ....)

6. What is an impervious surface?

Impervious surfaces block and prevent water from absorbing into the soil. These surfaces include driveways, rooftops, sidewalks, asphalt or concrete roads, and parking lots just to name a few. Water flows rapidly on impervious surfaces, hindering soil absorption and increasing water runoff. With rainstorms and snow melts, these impervious surfaces channel water that eventually ends up in our creeks, streams, and lakes. This affects the soils by both erosion and, possibly, contamination from chemicals. Refer back to chapter three for additional information.

7. What about mineral, oil, and gas rights?

The rights to minerals, oils, or gases that could be extracted from the property are often sold or leased to businesses or individuals. This is called mining. If the property contains natural resources, you should make sure the rights are intact with the land and not sold or leased out prior to a land purchase.

To fully research this, you need to have a mineral abstract or a mineral title opinion performed, usually by an attorney. A mineral abstract/title opinion is an

in-depth title search that researches the property facts on record many years back specifically for anything related to mineral, gas, or oil rights that would affect the title to the land. There are different types of abstracts depending on the situation, and it can be a costly process. Your intended use will let you know whether you want to spend the money and time with an attorney to research this in detail.[56 57]

Often, builders/developers will test the soils not only for contamination but for rock, soil, and structures, as well as employ ground-penetrating radar (GPR), which uses high-frequency radio waves. Frequently, builders or developers do not realize the depth and width of a vein of rock and spend a lot of money blasting, hammering, and removing the rock to make the soils usable and buildable. That unexpected expense eats up a large part of the profit for the project.[58]

8. What is radon gas?

Radon is an odorless, colorless, radioactive gas made from naturally decaying uranium in rocks and soil. It can enter homes through the soil and get trapped in the home by seeping through porous concrete and gaps in a home's walls and floors. Long-term exposure to high levels of radon gas has been known to cause lung cancer.[59]

Who tests for radon gas?

You can hire a radon mitigation expert to test for radon gas. You can also purchase kits to test for

yourself, but I recommend using a professional if you have any concerns. Many home inspection companies offer this service as well.

> **NOTE:** Did you know that radon gas at low levels is found in the air we breathe every day? It can also be found in underground and surface water.

Are radon levels higher in certain areas of the country?

To better see where in the country the radon levels seem to be more concentrated, check out the website for the US Environmental Protection Agency (EPA); they have a radon zones map.[60]

Conclusion

I hope you now have a better idea of why soil testing is so important when purchasing land. If you buy land that has bad soils, guess what? It may be unusable for you or your client's intended use. You must consider what the use for the property will be and go from there. Most of you reading this book are residential agents, and it is mainly for you I wrote this book. I want to help you avoid the mistakes that I—and other agents and the general public—have made in the past just because I didn't know what to consider with soils and land. Soils also play a major role with wells and septic systems as you will see in our next important chapter.

“There is no substitute for experience.”[61]

–Marilyn L. Rice

"All the water that will ever be is, right now."[62]

–National Geographic

8

Water and Sewer/ Well and Septic

Story: What are the white spots?

I purchased a home on an acre of land out in the country near my folks. Of course, it was on well and septic, which is mostly what I am used to. Several homes that I have owned in my life have been on well and septic systems. When I purchased this particular home, I suspected there might be a water issue because of the white-looking water spots around the kitchen sink; I have seen this many times. Silly me, I should have had the water tested prior to closing—I knew better! This is also an issue my folks have dealt with over the past forty years at their home. I just didn't know how bad it was. Anyway, I closed and started renovations. Since I was not living in the home during renovations, I did not realize the seriousness of the water issues. I had installed a new

kitchen faucet and within the first few days, I started noticing the white water spots around the faucet and on my glassware in the dishwasher. I also noticed the water had a smell. Shortly after that, one of my water heaters quit heating the water. Why? Because the hard water had covered and eaten a large hole in the heating element. I had the water tested, and although there was no contamination, the water hardness was off the charts. I had to purchase and install a water-softening system. Shortly after installation, all was well (no pun intended). There were no more smells, no more white spots, and the system was very easy to maintain. All I had to do for this type of system was add a bag of salt crystals once a month. That's it for me, and it's a piece of cake. I have great water and no more corrosion or spots on my appliances, pipes, sinks, or toilets. Problem solved.

Since I love the taste of well water and the ease of septic tanks, this is the norm for me. I also do not like paying for water or sewer, so a well and septic tank is perfect. Just one less bill to deal with. Do not be afraid of a home with well and septic systems; you may grow to love them. However, do remember to have the water tested even if it's on county/city water; it is just good to know what is in the water you drink. In this chapter, we'll explore issues related to water and sewer systems and well and septic systems. This topic should become a standard part of your research for land and lot sales.

What is the difference between water and sewer and well and septic?

One of the first things you should check when you begin researching a property is to determine the utilities. Does the property have access to water and sewer or use well and septic? It is possible it could have both.

Water you consume in a residence or building either comes from the water supply maintained by the county or city and is piped to each home or business, or it is pumped from a drilled well located on the property.

Sewer lines are also provided by the county or city and use underground pipes that direct wastewater to a treatment facility maintained by the county or city, whereas septic systems are underground holding tanks combined with leach fields installed on the property.

1. Water and sewer (typically public utilities)

Water and sewer services installed and provided by the county or city are referred to as public utilities and have associated monthly fees. In some areas, there are also private companies that supply the water and sewer utilities for a monthly fee.

In some cases, a private developer of a proposed housing or commercial development may be required to install the utility lines and connect them to public services. This installation could require easements to be obtained from nearby property owners to allow the water or sewer lines to be constructed across their property. This can improve property values for many

homes or businesses in the area that would then be able to connect to the county-maintained lines.

When dealing with land, one of the first questions that arises is the subject of the sewer. Is the sewer gravity-fed, or will the sewer line require a pump? What is the difference? A gravity-fed sewer line is just as it sounds. Gravity allows the waste to flow downhill through the sewer lines naturally. A pump on the other hand allows homes or structures to be placed on a property below the natural gravity line. The pump is used to push the waste to the main sewer line for dispersal. These systems, for a single lot, normally use what is called a grinder pump to turn the solid waste into a sludge material to allow for easier pumping through the pipes. However, for a large tract of land to be developed, a pump station may be required. Depending on the size of the development, these pump stations can be rather large in order to handle the waste dispersal for an entire subdivision.

On a separate note, you may want to take into consideration that adding a pump to a sewer system will obviously increase the cost of the infrastructure of the property. If it is a single lot, it could be a relatively small amount of money. Depending on the area in which you are researching you will need to investigate the costs during your inspection period. If it is a large tract to be developed, it could add several hundred thousand dollars to infrastructure costs. This cost will need to be investigated during your due diligence or inspection period and should be considered during your research of land, as it may affect an offer to a seller.

If you determine the property you are researching has access to public utilities, you should identify the location of the water and sewer lines closest to the property. You can do this by calling the public works or the utility department to find the nearest locations. You will be asked for the parcel ID number or an address of the property in order for them to locate the site.

> **NOTE:** Confirm there is capacity available to serve the property. Just because there is water and sewer at or near the property does not mean that you will be able to connect. The city/county utilities only allow so many properties to connect based on the availability of the service and its capacity to handle the service. You must check availability of each service separately. A "tap fee" may be required, so you may want to ask the cost prior to scheduling service.

2. Well and septic (typically private utilities)

If you are researching land in a rural area, it is likely there will be no public utilities for water and sewer available. In that case, you will need to consider well and septic for a structure.

Well and septic are typically located on the property where the structure or residence is located. These are maintained by the homeowner and are not connected to public utility services. A well's water comes from underlying aquifers (from groundwater) brought to the surface through drilling. The water is then piped into the home for human consumption. From the home, the used water or wastewater (effluent) goes into the septic

tank, and maybe a pump tank, where it is dispersed back into the soils. Rural land that has no access to public water or sewer lines will require installation of well and septic systems if the intent is to build a home or structure that is to have bedrooms. Once the well and septic systems are installed and in use, you typically will not have to pay a monthly fee for water, but you may or may not pay additional septic fees—except in some states where a septic system maintenance contract may be required to maintain the septic system. Check your local government agency to see which septic system may or may not require a septic system maintenance contract.

As the county or city develops and installs utility services accessible to the property, the property owner may have an option to "tap on" or "hook up" to the public utility lines for a fee. The property owner might decide to keep the well for irrigation and add the water line for the building consumption. However, if the property owners decide they do not want to hook onto the water or sewer line, it could be more expensive to tap on later. You will need to confirm options with the local government.

A consideration for wells to keep in mind is if you have a well as your primary source of drinking water, pay attention to any construction nearby as it can affect the water underground in ways that are above my understanding. Also, if you are in the country setting and a nearby farmer is spreading manure from animals on his fields for fertilizer, you really want to have your well tested regularly for its potability for human consumption.

> **NOTE:** I encourage testing the well water for contaminants and other health concerns before assuming it is safe for human consumption prior to closing on a property.

3. What is a septic system?

A septic system serves the same purpose as public sewer lines—removing wastewater from homes and buildings—but may or may not be contained within the parcel boundaries. It may consist of several underground treatment tanks installed near the structure to receive, hold, and disperse all of the wastewater from bathrooms, kitchens, and washing machines.

Soil suitability tests or percolation (perc) tests are important in determining if the soils are suitable for wastewater and within county guidelines. These results will help determine the location of and distance from the wells and where the structure will be placed on the property. Proper distance between well and septic is vital in preventing contamination of the well water. In our community it is anywhere from fifty feet to one hundred feet minimum. The type of septic systems, their locations, and, if applicable, the distance of setbacks from wells will change based on the perc test and your particular county requirements.

The county will require a septic permit for installation of any septic system, and it remains on file at the county courthouse. The permit displays an illustration of the septic tank and lines and where they are located on the property in relation to any structure or proposed structure. If you are purchasing

a property that has an existing septic system in place, you can request a copy of the permit from the county.

How does a septic system work?
A typical septic system is designed to receive all water (from a washing machine, sink, shower, toilet, etc.) or wastewater, from the residence. From the residence, the effluent flows into one of two compartments in the septic tank (one side of the tank for solids and liquids and the other side for liquids only) that are separated by a baffle wall inside the tank. These tanks are traditionally concrete. However, polyethylene or fiberglass tanks are available options. In the first compartment of the septic tank, gravity settles the solids to the bottom of the tank, and they become sludge. For the most part, the liquids overflow through the baffle wall and into the second compartment of the septic tank and typically disperse back into the ground into individual septic drain lines. These combined septic drain lines are referred to as drain fields or leach fields and allow the effluent to be absorbed back into the soil and digested by the microbes in the soil. The leach fields are 100+ feet of buried pipes, depending on the number of bedrooms the system would support.The solids, on the other hand, accumulate in the septic tank and eventually reach the tank's storage capacity. At that point, the tank will require servicing to be pumped out by a septic contractor.

Depending on the type of system you have and its frequency of use, a septic inspection will determine

how often a tank may need to be serviced. When a system is in need of service, the property owner should hire a septic pumping company to vacuum or pump out the septic tank. The technician will uncover the septic tank lids, remove the inlet side of the septic tank lid, and vacuum out the solids.

4. Common types of septic systems

There are many types of septic systems available depending on the circumstances of the property. The most common systems are:

Conventional septic system

With a conventional system, wastewater from the septic tank or pump tank (effluent typically being pumped up to a higher elevation) is then dispersed into the drain lines and absorbed into the ground by gravity. Once the in-ground tank is filled with solids and liquids, the tank effluent will slowly drain to a smaller concrete box called a distribution box (or D-box) or directly into the individual septic lines. The D-box device distributes the effluent water into a number of drain lines that make up the drain field.

Conventional pump system

Due to the property elevations, sometimes a conventional pump system is required. This is a conventional septic system with an added pump feature to pump the effluent to a higher elevation. The effluent is then dispersed into the drain lines and then absorbed into the ground by gravity.

Low-pressure pipe pump system

In less-than-perfect ground conditions, where you only have the option of a shallow drain field, a low-pressure system may be used. These systems typically use small pumps that force the effluent through an array of PVC pipes with varying-diameter drain holes. These systems might require more maintenance with septic contracts. In some cases, low-pressure pipe septic systems are used for deep soil.[63]

Clearly it is important to know what kind of utility access you have or will need, whether that means you need sewer access or a septic system, and what the water accessibility is or will need to be. When dealing with a septic system, remember your hired soil scientist will be able to tell you the kind of system you will be required to install; this is not something you will need to guess on your own. Obviously by now, you know the soils will determine this for you. And please take the drinking water seriously and have it tested. These are also important facts to know when purchasing in a neighborhood. There may be rules and regulations in the HOA and CC&Rs regarding your well and septic or your water and sewer access; you never know until you read the documents, hopefully prior to your purchase. Let's take a look at that in the next chapter.

"In the middle of every difficulty lies opportunity."[64]

–Albert Einstein

"I never had a policy; I just tried to do my very best each and every day."[65]

–Abraham Lincoln

Community Restrictions

Story: Where is my boat?

I have an acquaintance who worked with the daughter of one of his best buddies, and she was a new real estate agent (new as in: the ink was still wet on her real estate license). He wanted to help her out, so he engaged her services to help him purchase a condo in an older, upscale neighborhood next to the golf community of which he was a member. I say older because the homes were the contemporary home styles of the '80s, but people were purchasing them and spending a lot of money gutting them to update the style of the interior. The location was A+, near a country club setting, so the purchase was a good investment since he was of retirement age and ready to just travel and have fun.

The purchase went smoothly and he started renovations. The renovations were going to be top-notch and expensive just to renovate the interior of the unit. He used the best of everything right down to the decking, which cost him several thousand dollars for a small deck on the back of this ground-level condo. That's when he got his first notice that he needed to remove and replace the entire new deck because it did not meet the color standards. By the way, no one could see the deck except him (the owner) and one other neighbor, who happened to love the new deck. So, he begged and pleaded with the HOA president and board members, but you know how that goes with an HOA board sometimes. Upon a thorough reading of the HOA and CC&Rs, he would have discovered that he needed approval for his deck color prior to installation.

So, he did as was required and removed the expensive new deck, replaced it with a different color, and kept on with the amazing renovations. This place looked like something out of an uptown magazine, top-of-the-line everything.

He moved in, and all was well for the first few days. Until he walked out of the front door and said, "Where is my boat?" He had plenty of room in his drive for his boat, his car was in the garage, and his truck to pull the boat was right beside the boat in the driveway. You know where this story is going. The HOA had his boat towed. Had he and his agent done their homework, he would have realized—by thoroughly reading the HOA and CC&Rs documents—that he could not

park anything in the driveway other than his personal vehicle. He was hot, and I mean his temper, and now he had to locate his expensive boat and then find a place to park it outside of the neighborhood.

So, remember this story and find out what your clients' needs are, then read the HOA and CC&R documents prior to making an offer or at least early on during the inspection or due diligence period. This could save everyone a lot of headaches. And don't forget to ask your clients if they will need extra parking for any current or future purchases. They may have plans you are not aware of. On the other hand, if your clients need land for all of their toys, make sure the local ordinances allow the use of the property for their desires. For example, what if they are gun enthusiasts and like to shoot on their own property—say, target shooting? Check the local ordinances to make sure it is okay. Where I grew up it was okay, and now it is not. My daddy is not happy, go figure ... things change and so do ordinances. We even have to get a burn permit to burn yard debris now. Crazy stuff!

1. What is an HOA?

HOAs, or homeowners associations, are usually formed by real estate developers for the purpose of managing and regulating the covenants, conditions, and restrictions (CC&Rs) for homes and lots in residential subdivisions. After a predetermined percentage of the homes are sold, the developer releases control of the homeowners association to the residents.

An elected HOA board of directors enforces the rules and guidelines for the subdivision, community, or condominium building. These associations typically require individual homeowners to pay an annual or monthly fee to maintain common areas. Examples of common areas are entrances to the neighborhoods, landscaping, playgrounds, and community pools, which are all used by the entire neighborhood and are governed by the CC&Rs.

If the parcel of land or lot you are researching is in a neighborhood, you will need to determine whether or not it has an HOA. You may have to contact the county's register of deeds office to get a copy of the HOA's rules and guidelines, which should have been recorded with the county. Another option is to ask residents who live in the subdivision for the name and phone number of the neighborhood's HOA president. Often, HOAs have a neighborhood website.[66]

When reviewing HOA documents, look for the following items:

- CC&Rs
- rules and regulations
- bylaws
- financials
- meeting minutes

2. What are CC&Rs?

Covenants, conditions, and restrictions (CC&Rs) are rules put in place by the developer that regulate a neighborhood or development, whether residential or commercial. CC&Rs tell you what you can and

cannot do in a neighborhood. If the land or lot is in a neighborhood, you should research to see if any CC&Rs are in place and recorded at the courthouse.

CC&Rs may specify some of the following:

- building materials and exterior colors
- landscaping and lighting
- parking limitations
- exterior fencing and outbuildings
- minimum/maximum square footage per house
- setbacks

Within a majority of residential neighborhoods, a proposed house or changes to an existing property will have to go through an architectural review board (ARB) for approvals. The ARB will follow the guidelines set up in the CC&Rs. You can get a copy of the CC&Rs at the county's register of deeds office.

On a separate note, as solar power becomes more popular, it is a good topic to address when helping a client purchase a home. Neighborhood restrictions can prohibit solar panels in a neighborhood to preserve the look of the neighborhood.

Caution: Just because a neighborhood has no HOA does not mean there are no CC&Rs.[67]

3. Where can you locate HOA and CC&R documents? HOA and CC&R documents should be recorded at your local county assessor's office, recorder's office, or register of deeds office along with any amendments made to the HOAs and CC&Rs over the years. The name of the neighborhood and the road

on which it is located is all you need. You may be able to find these through a real estate agent who is a member of the local MLS (multiple listing service). Many MLS organizations have HOA and CC&R documents online.[68]

4. What are deed restrictions, and how are they enforced with regards to a neighborhood and their CC&Rs?

Deed restrictions limit the use of land and are placed in a deed between private parties but are enforced by a homeowners association or local governments. For additional information about deed restrictions, refer to chapter six.

5. Who is responsible for researching deed restrictions?

An attorney or title company is typically employed to research deeds and deed restrictions. However, you and your buyer should always read over the deed restrictions yourself. An attorney can interpret a deed and restrictions, but it is not the attorney's job to apply it to your specific requirements. It could be something simple, such as not being able to park a boat or an RV in a driveway or neighborhood. Better to know ahead of time rather than after you have closed and moved in.

> **NOTE:** If you are representing a buyer on a lot in a subdivision, read the CC&Rs ***with*** the buyer prior to making an offer to make sure the CC&Rs align with the buyer's expectations. My suggestion is to err on the side of caution and hire an attorney to interpret the CC&Rs first.

The HOAs and CC&Rs are put in place to help maintain the look and value of a neighborhood. These rules are actually a good thing, as people may interpret them based on their knowledge and its relativity to them. One homeowner may interpret them entirely differently than another. That is why they elect a board to manage the guidelines set in place for the neighborhood—so that everyone is on the same page. I said earlier in the chapter, do your homework for yourself or your clients before you even go to the trouble to write up an offer. If you have questions, contact the HOA president to help you understand. This leads us into the next most important chapter—location! Yep, it's finally here, the location of where to live or own property and the many things to take into consideration before you begin your search for land. Why? Because just about everything sits on land.

"You just can't beat the person who won't give up."[69]

–Babe Ruth

10 Land Locations: Last but Not Least?

Story: A determined Thirsty Beaver ...

There is a small, local bar in downtown Charlotte, North Carolina called the Thirsty Beaver. The landlord of this little one-story iconic bar refused to sell to a developer in a large land purchase surrounding the bar on all sides but the street front. The development was for a large proposed apartment complex in this very popular growing community of young professionals. The owner of the establishment along with the landlord of the property stood firm to maintain what had become an iconic local hangout in the Charlotte area since 2008. After the developer made many attempts to purchase, relocate, and even intimidate the duo into selling or moving, the property owner and tenant remained firm on keeping a little part of Charlotte from being swallowed up. As of the

writing of this book, the Thirsty Beaver is surrounded by an apartment building with more than 320 units on three sides, and the "little bar that stood" still has its charm and clientele. Sometimes money is not everything, but what matters is location and a whole lot of heart.

Image is author's own.

The Thirsty Beaver Saloon, 2020

You've heard it said many times: "Location, location, location!" Here's why. It is true when it comes to property values that location matters! This is why knowing and understanding the location of the property and what is happening in the surrounding area is so important.

Agents should research a property in depth. However, understanding the key elements of a particular location is vital for determining if the property is right for your client. Some examples are:

- If a future road is proposed, the noise could be too much to bear.
- If someone has children, the school system and neighborhood will be of top concern.
- If the clients are elderly, proximity to medical services may be important.
- If buyers require shopping convenience, that must be addressed.
- If someone works from home, access to the internet and mobile services will be a priority.
- If someone travels frequently for business, access to airports may be desirable.
- If someone has utility preferences (such as for natural gas or city water/sewer versus well/septic), this will be important to know.
- If the client has certain requests or requirements in a neighborhood, then you'll want to find a neighborhood that will match your client's needs.

1. Future roads

Future roads can impact the value of a property in a positive or negative way depending on the new road's location, function, and purpose. For residential locations, increased volume of drive-through traffic along with noise pollution can negatively affect a neighborhood's property value. However, in some

cases, new roads can provide better access in rural areas, enhancing the property value or making way for future development. New roads that increase traffic can provide easier access and greater visibility, which affect a commercial site in a positive way. The addition of new roads and improved traffic flow can be of economic benefit by attracting more commercial properties along the new road and providing additional services to the communities. Major road developments—such as a bypass road—could divert traffic away from a particular area. This rerouting of traffic could have an adverse effect on local businesses by creating financial hardship within a community through loss of employment opportunities.

It is vital to be informed of proposed new roads as well as improvements to existing roads! You can check with your state's local department of transportation or the county planning department office to learn more.

Roads in a neighborhood

If you are considering purchasing a lot in a neighborhood, check to see whether the roads are public or private. Repair and maintenance of public roads is managed by the county and state. However, roads in a gated residential community are privately owned and maintained by the HOA and paid for out of the annual dues or special assessments.

An assessment is an additional expense to a community for infrequent or unexpected maintenance or improvements to a property operating under a HOA. The cost of the assessment typically covers what

is normally not covered by annual HOA dues, and the added cost of the assessment is divided equally among each unit within the development.

Assessments are neighborhood specific and can be costly depending on the circumstances. By reviewing the HOA's financial statements prior to considering a purchase, you may be able to discover any existing or potential future assessments.

You can find more information in the article "When HOA Associations Can Impose Special Assessments" by Beth Ross.[70]

2. Schools

Many young couples and growing families seek locations based on the quality of the schools in a particular area. To better assist your buyer, become familiar with surrounding public and private schools, as well as available preschools and daycares. Call the county school system or access the county website with the address or street/road name of the property. Most public school systems have assignment look-ups on their county school websites. Additionally, GIS websites may also have public school assignments easily accessible by using the Schools Layer tab.

> **NOTE:** Always verify school assignments to ensure they are correct. Do not trust MLS data. Better yet, have your clients verify school assignments.

3. Hospitals

Whether old or young, proximity to hospitals and medical services may be desired. Researching the area for existing and future medical locations and providers will help you become more knowledgeable of the area and better able to assist your clients.

4. Fire stations and rescue squads

The location of emergency help is especially important to the elderly and parents with smaller children. Fire stations and rescue locations can also affect the cost of homeowners insurance. When searching for land in a rural setting, you will need to know how far away the fire station is in relation to a property. This is just good information to share with your buyer.

Fire Hydrants

Not all homeowners consider where their property is in relation to fire hydrants, but this is a good thing to know. Not only is it a benefit should you have a fire emergency, but your insurance could be less expensive. Property located near a fire hydrant is less likely to be engulfed in flames, which could minimize damage to the property and the expense to the insurance company. In a rural setting, you will be hard-pressed to find fire hydrants, so know the location or distance to the nearest fire station as mentioned above.

5. Shopping

Many consider shopping convenience a priority, while others dislike the traffic conditions surrounding large-scale shopping centers. This is potentially the easiest

thing to learn about an area, but you will also want to research any plans for new developments. Contact the local county planning department to discover if there are any proposed projects in the works.

6. Cell towers and internet coverage

Many, if not all, people now rely on cell tower use and internet access. Your clients may desire a beautiful home in a rural country setting, but if it will be years before they have internet access, you will need to know this before making an offer on a property. Likewise, there are still many areas that do not have cell towers for mobile phone connectivity. Do your homework. Find out who the carriers are for that area.

> **NOTE**: Contact all utility companies to confirm they service the area you are researching.

7. Water and sewer locations

Chapter eight covered a lot of information on the importance and location of water and sewer and use of well and septic. Confirm if there are water and sewer locations and sources for the property being considered by your client or if your client will be required to install and maintain well and septic.

8. Electricity

Do not take electricity for granted! A quick internet search using the zip code followed by "power company" will determine which power companies service the area. You will then need to contact each

company to confirm whether they provide service to the location of interest.

9. Natural or propane gas

Some clients prefer natural gas over electric for heating and some appliances. A simple call to the local gas company will determine if there are natural gas lines nearby or if the property will need to have a propane tank installed on site.

10. Airports and interstate locations

If frequent travel is important to a buyer, the distance to the closest airport or interstate might be a strong determining factor in the purchase of a property, whether residential or commercial. Conversely, be aware of the air traffic patterns over the property.

11. Neighborhood dynamics

Ultimately, a neighborhood's dynamic will add to the homeowners' overall quality of life. Understanding your clients and knowing their interests will guide you in finding the neighborhood or community that is perfect for them ... or it may just be "the little house on the prairie" that suits their needs.

Things to observe are:

- Is it a peaceful, quiet community where everyone respects each other's privacy and keeps to themselves?
- Is it a friendly sidewalk community perfect for walking, strolling, and socializing with neighbors?

- Does it have amenities—such as, sports fields, playgrounds, or swimming pools—suitable for active families?
- Is your client mature in age but ready for an active lifestyle community with less home maintenance and more social involvement? This can be a tricky topic for a broker. Be careful not to violate any fair housing laws.
- Is it obvious the residents take pride of ownership and cleanliness of their homes, yards, and common areas?
- Does the area offer a genuine feeling of safety and security by way of speed limitations, community watch programs, and local police presence?

Taking the time to first understand your client, wants and needs and then implementing these desires to locate the right property will save you and them a great deal of time. After all, we only have twenty-four hours in a day, and you can spend it all hauling them around and hoping you'll come upon the right one. Take a little of that time and do your homework with questions and research first. Knowing their desires upfront, like what are the top three most important factors in finding their perfect land or home location, will make your job so much easier. Keep these things in mind as you do your research. Writing them down keeps me on track.

Conclusion

I know this book was more than ten things, but I really wanted you all to know how much I care about teaching you information that I had to learn the hard way. I hope you feel that this is a book of great value. You can share what you've learned from this book with potential clients, and they will see that you know your stuff. Honestly, I have found that working with an educated client makes my job so much more fun, not to mention easier. Sometimes they teach *you* things! So, gift this book to as many clients as you think you can handle. They may feel obligated to use you as they will see that you are trying to help them make an educated decision, instead of making just another commision. Gifting is a wonderful thing, and people don't forget generosity. It is a small investment upfront that can have a large payout in the end. Thanks for taking the time to purchase, read, and share this book! I have a few bonus goodies for you to think about ahead that I also feel are helpful tips and resources.

> ***"For every sale you miss because you're too enthusiastic, you will miss a hundred because you're not enthusiastic enough."***
>
> –Zig Ziglar[71]

New Observations about Land

Regardless of your motivation to know more about land, you should now be viewing land through a different lens. No matter who you are or what land means to you, the importance of research and knowing your resources is critical. As an investor, every deal is different, so knowing a property's potential can be more lucrative if you do your research. As a landowner or maybe someone who recently inherited land, it is important to know your property's value. If you are a residential agent pursuing land transactions, understanding the complexities of raw property will set you apart from the competition.

As you pursue your interest in land, whatever that may be, you should begin to look at it in a new and different way.

When you look at a piece of land, what do you see?

- Is it usable land? Is it suitable for a structure?
- Is it wooded? Is there timber to be harvested or that is suitable for homes?
- Is it a meadow? Does it have the potential to be a neighborhood or farmland?
- Is there a pond, lake, or creek? Could it be an amenity for a subdivision or a park?
- Is it a farm or does it have rolling hills? Can it be used for livestock or hunting land?
- Is there a lot of dirt, and what is the quality of the soils? Is it industrial or a gravel pit?
- Is it commercial? Are there shopping centers or parking garage potentials?
- Does it have high-density residential potential? Could it be an apartment site or maybe townhomes?
- Is it near railroads or floodplains? Is it industrial or unusable land?
- Is the land in the path of growth? Is a future road coming to or through the property?

Being observant of your surroundings during your daily routine can uncover potential opportunities. Watch for movement and activity, posts for rezoning, newly placed survey stakes, utility installations, For Sale signs, and land clearing or timbering, to name a few. In addition to your observations, attend your local town hall meetings, talk to friends and neighbors, be a good listener, and be available.

There are many things mentioned in this book to be aware of when researching land. One thing not mentioned is how to value a property. This is not an easy task in and of itself. There are many factors that go into deciding the value of land, and I wish that I could give you a magic formula to use on all land. Each parcel has its own benefits and drawbacks, and you as an agent will need to take into consideration all of these facts when pricing a property for sale. Recent comparisons will definitely help you, but everything that sells is not necessarily on the local multiple listing service. You may have to visit your local municipality and research some records or use the GIS to see if you can locate some recent, nearby sales to help you in determining the value.

County/City Department Resources

If the GIS fails in providing the information you are researching, here's the secret: Ask! Ask! Ask! All of this information is available to the public. Do not be afraid to make the call and ask the questions in pursuit of answers. Most government employees are very helpful. Here is a go-to list of county and city departments and what information they can provide.

The tax assessor's office can tell you:

- who owns the property
- the amount of taxes paid or owed
- the location of the deed reference to the property
- the number of acres
- the value of the property

- in which municipality (town/city) the property is located,
- if the property is in a farm program, and
- exclusions for elderly or disabled persons or veterans.

The register of deeds office can provide you with:

- the owner's name(s)
- the deeds to the property
- mortgage information and HOAs and CC&Rs that are recorded
- fixture filings (swimming pools, for example)
- land records (deeds/surveys/plats)
- POA (power of attorney) documents, and
- certificates of assumed names for business.

The clerk of court or county recorder's office (depending on the state) can tell you about:

- wills (if they are recorded)
- estate files (such as probate)
- foreclosures, and
- liens.

The planning and zoning department can tell you about:

- the subdivision of land
- zoning and rezoning
- transportation
- flood plains
- future land use plans, and
- ordinances.

Public works/utilities/engineering departments can provide information on:

- water and sewer line locations in relation to the property you are researching, and whether or not it is accessible and if it has available capacity.
- well and septic systems. Contact the environmental department to get a procedure list on moving forward with well and septic installations.

During your research and while making your calls, it can be helpful to gather all of your information in one place. I have provided my personal Land Information Sheet as well as a Need to Know Checklist in the back of the book for your use or reference. Feel free to make copies and use them as-is or create some of your own. Additionally, visit my website to download a free copy of either (www.cherylsain.com).

"If you always do what you've always done, you'll always get what you've always got."[72]

–Jessie Potter

What Now?

You are the best investment you can make! We never stop learning. By choosing to read *10 Things You Need to Know About Land*, you are investing in yourself by improving your knowledge and becoming better equipped to help yourself and others. If you only take away one piece of information or idea from this book, I hope it is the importance of thoroughly doing your research and knowing your resources.

I hope that by reading this book, you real estate agents/brokers, landowners, or investors now have a better understanding of what you need to know about a lot or raw land when the opportunity comes your way. Whether it be in land, real estate, or just life, I hope I was able to guide you through some situations that either you had not thought about or you wished you had known earlier. My goal was to help you feel better equipped to deal with different land scenarios and to, hopefully, contribute even in the smallest way to your future success.

Now go and ... do real good things today!

"Formal education gets you a job, but self-education is what makes you rich!"[73]

–Jim Rohn

Recommended Reading

For a deeper understanding of land and commercial real estate, I recommend the following programs or books:

Land and commercial real estate

- Realtor Land Institute (www.rliland.com)
- Certified Commercial Investment Member (www.ccim.com)
- ArcGIS, a mapping and analytical program, (arcgis.com or www.esri.com)

Self-improvement

To help you in your journey to grow—whatever that looks like for you—here are a few books that I recommend, and not in any particular order. Remember that you are in sales, management, and negotiations every day and in most everything you do in life.

1. **The Holy Bible**
2. Bancroft, Jonathan, and Roy H. Williams. **Mr. Jenkins Told Me … Forgotten Principles That Will Grow Any Business.** Austin, TX: Wizard Academy Press, 2019.
3. Blanchard, Ken, and Spencer Johnson. **The New One Minute Manager.** New York: William Morrow, 2015.
4. Canfield, Jack. **The Success Principles.** New York: William Morrow, 2015.
5. Carnegie, Dale. **How to Win Friends and Influence People.** New York: Simon & Schuster, 2011.
6. Cialdini, Robert B. **Influence: The Psychology of Persuasion.** New York: Harper Business, 2006.
7. Hill, Napoleon. **Think and Grow Rich.** New York: TarcherPerigree, 2005.
8. Klaff, Oren. **Pitch Anything.** New York: McGraw-Hill, 2011.
9. McRaven, William H. **Make Your Bed.** New York: Grand Central Publishing, 2017.
10. Nierenberg, Roger. **Maestro: A Surprising Story About Leading by Listening.** New York: Portfolio, 2009.
11. Patterson, Kerry, Joseph Grenny, Ron McMillan, and Al Switzler. **Crucial Confrontations: Tools for Resolving Broken Promises, Violated Expectations, and Bad Behavior.** New York: McGraw-Hill, 2004.

12. Patterson, Kerry, Joseph Grenny, Ron McMillan, and Al Switzler. **Crucial Conversations: Tools for Talking When Stakes Are High.** New York: McGraw-Hill, 2011.
13. Pennington, Loyd. **Change One Word, Change Your Life.** Windermere, FL: Pennington/Acquire, 2015.
14. Porter, Pat. **Land Buying Tips from the Pros.** Scotts Valley, CA: Createspace Independent Publishing Platform, 2016.
15. Voss, Chris. **Never Split the Difference: Negotiating as if Your Life Depended on It.** London: Random House UK, 2017.
16. Any book written by Jim Rohn.
17. Any book written by Zig Ziglar.

Websites:

1. ArcGIS, Mapping and Analytical Program. Accessed Aug. 1, 2020. www.arcgis.com or www.esri.com.
2. Certified Commercial Investment Member. Accessed Aug. 1, 2020. www.ccim.com.
3. Realtors Land Institute. Accessed Aug. 1, 2020. www.rliland.com.

“Whether you think you can or think you can’t, you’re right!”[74]

–Henry Ford

10 Things You Need to Know Checklist

1. Parcel ID number
2. Owner's name and address
3. Discovering land conditions
4. Parcel deed
5. Survey
6. Parcel zoning and density
7. Soils
8. Water and sewer or well and septic location
9. Community restrictions, HOAs, and CC&Rs
10. Importance of land locations

For a free download of this Need to Know Checklist, visit my website:

www.cherylsain.com

10 Things You Need to Know Land Information Sheet

Client contact date:____________________________

Property location/parcel ID number: ____________

____

Property owner's name/address: ____________________

____

Municipality and/or county: ____________________

____

Water: well or county/city: ______________________

____

Waterline location in relation to property: ________

____

Water taps installed and/or paid (yes/no): ________

Sewer or septic: ______________________________

Sewer taps installed and/or paid (yes/no): _________

Utilities to property (yes/no): __________________

Easements (yes/no):______________________________

Current zoning and density: ____________________

____

Flood plain on property (yes/no): ________________

Current survey (yes/no): ________________________

Have a copy of deed (yes/no): ___________________

Any due diligence material (yes/no): _____________

Any soils information (yes/no): __________________

Mortgages (yes/no): ____________________________

Liens (yes/no): ________________________________

HOA and CC&Rs (yes/no): _____________________

Current site approvals (yes/no): _________________

Elementary school and ratings: __________________

____

Middle school and ratings: _____________________

____

High school and ratings: _______________________

____

Seller/owners or buyer contact information

(circle one): Seller Owner

Agent contact information: _____________________

____

____

LOI (letter of intent/interest) submittal date: ______

____

LOI execution date: ___________________________

Contract submittal date: _______________________

Contract execution date: _______________________

Buyer's attorney: ______________________________

Buyer's attorney's phone/email: __________________

____

Buyer's attorney's address: _____________________

____

____

Seller's attorney: ______________________________

Seller's attorney's phone/email: __________________

____

Seller's attorney's address: _____________________

____

____

Earnest money deposit (EMD) due: ______________

EMD deposited (yes/no): _______________________

Due diligence deposit due: _____________________

Due diligence / inspection period ends: __________

Extensions (yes/no): __________________________

Extension executed date: _______________________

Closing date: _________________________________

For a free download of this Land Information Sheet, visit my website:

www.cherylsain.com

Land Glossary

Contour lines—Lines on a map that are used to determine elevations. They are produced from connecting points of equal elevation.

Deed stamps—This is a one-time tax at the time a property is sold and the deed is submitted to the county for recording.

Deed of trust—This is an agreement between a lender and a borrower that allows a third party to serve as a trustee until the borrower pays off the debt.

Easement—This gives someone permission or the right to use or cross someone else's land for a specific purpose.

Lien—A lien on real estate is when a creditor attaches a notice to the property claiming the owner owes money to the creditor. This is a way for a creditor to collect what he or she is owed when a property changes ownership.

Lot—A piece of land owned by an individual or entity. It could be improved, meaning water and/or sewer and/or utilities are in place. We mostly think of a lot in a subdivision (a parcel of land divided into many smaller parcels to form lots for houses to be built on) when we hear the word "lot" referring to land. A lot can also refer to a commercial outparcel in commercial development, as in a shopping center.

Perc test—These tests determine the soil's ability to accept effluent (wastewater) over a period of time.

Plat—A map of a land area, such as a neighborhood.

Plot—A piece of land used for a single purpose, such as a home.

Potable water—Water that can be consumed without concern for adverse health effects. Non-potable water is unsafe for human consumption.

Prescriptive easements—An easement by which a person's real property is acquired by continued use by another person without permission of the legal owner of the property for a certain period of time. This may also be referred to as "adverse possession."

Raw land—Land in its natural state, with no man-made improvements and no livable structure.

Real property—Land and anything attached to it, built on it, or growing on it.

Title—In real estate, we refer to a title as the person or entity who has the legal ownership and right to use a property.

Topography (topo)—This is the lay of the land or the terrain. The topography is the mapping or charting of the shape and features of the land: Is it flat, or does it have rolling hills or mountains? A topographical description will determine what and where structures may be built on a parcel.

Acknowledgments

I am truly grateful for the many people who have inspired and encouraged me throughout my life and career in one memorable way or another.

Many thanks to the following professionals, family, and friends who have contributed valuable resources, information, and support to the writing of this book. I could not have done this without them.

Julie Holmes, for her complete confidence and support in me and my abilities to do just about anything. Her secret editing skills were irreplaceable in making this book what it has become, and I gladly share the "published book" title with her. Her endless hours of literally sitting by my side to edit this book and make it easier to understand were a priceless contribution. She has become a true lifelong friend and one of the most talented individuals I have ever met. Her help in molding this book is immeasurable.

Bill Gallagher, one of the best real estate educators of our time, for his thoughts, encouragement, and contributions to this book and his years of support and dedication through real estate education classes and endless laughs that made the learning fun in so many ways. Thank you.

Jim Lineberger, a long-time, devoted friend and broker for his content editing, cover contributions, and help in making this book what it has become. His persistence in closing the most difficult real estate deals I have ever encountered are unmatched.

Tim Bowes, 2019 president of the North Carolina Society of Surveyors, for his tremendous amount of critical information on one of my longest, more important chapters on surveying.

David Skidmore, a long-time survey friend, for his contributions to the survey chapter.

Kenny Owens, my go-to soil scientist buddy for his tremendous contributions to my soils and water and septic chapters.

Rick Harmon, my hydrogeologist go-to, for his contributions to several chapters in the book; I am so grateful.

A special thanks to attorneys Cathy Hunter and Clinton Chandler, whom I have known and respected through my entire real estate career, for their contributions to the deed chapter and for being examples of what attorneys really should be. It has been a pleasure knowing and working with you both through these many years of closings.

Sharon Browne, for her vast knowledge and persistence in making a real estate deal successful no matter the obstacles and for her contributions to the content of this project.

Ben Kuhn, Chellie Bennett, Bob Zito, Amanda Merrill, Gillian Baker, Bob Bunzey, Dr. Simon Ghanat, Saundra Quickle, Chesson Seagroves, Wanda Harrison, and Neal Pender for their story and content contributions.

Chad Lloyd, a long-time acquaintance in land acquisitions, for his contributions and encouragement during the writing and editing process.

Pat Porter, for his support and encouragement in my writing of this book. Thanks for the push and guidance; your books encouraged me to pursue my dream of helping others.

Tracy Sokol, my book and writing buddy, for her support and guidance in this journey of simultaneously writing our first books. Her commitment was admirable by any standard.

Jessica Newlin and Boo Hudson Courtney, for their lifelong friendships, love, and positive support with all of my ventures.

Loyd Pennington, Mike Baucom, and Laura Laire, for their positive outlook on life, for sharing the lessons we all need to learn, and for their never-ending desire to help others improve with good thoughts and deeds. Thank you for your support.

A special thank you to my editor Lindsey Alexander with The Reading List out of Chapel Hill, North Carolina, a jewel of a company.

And an exceptional thank you to my publishers Mindy Kuhn and Amy Ashby with Warren Publishing for their open-mindedness in design, layout, and marketing. Of course much thanks for their patience with this first-time author and my thousands of questions. I think we did something good, today.

Last but not least, Frances Davis, for being the best elementary school principal and mentor for whom a young lady could ever ask. She made a difference in this young girl's life, and I have never forgotten her and her belief in me.

**"In the end,
we only regret
the chances we
didn't take,
the relationships
we were afraid
to have, and the
decisions we waited
too long to make."**[75]

–Lewis Carroll

About the Author

Born and raised in the small rural town of Waxhaw, North Carolina with her younger brother Larry, Cheryl Sain grew up a tomboy with a girly streak, loving horses, dirt bikes, guns, animals, arts and crafts, and playing in the dirt—which is probably the source of her love for the land business.

In the early 1980s, after graduation from Sun Valley High School, she enlisted in the US Air Force to serve her country and as a means to afford a college education. Stationed in Myrtle Beach, South Carolina, her primary job in the air force was as an air traffic controller. After an honorable discharge from the Air Force, she stayed in the Air National Guard another three years.

Post Air Force, Cheryl became a successful stylist and owner of her own hair salon. Soon thereafter, a national hair and skin care company recruited her to become a tri-state regional manager with one of their primary distributors in Atlanta, Georgia. During this time, she met and married her husband. They remained in the Atlanta area until early 2000 when they returned to Charlotte, North Carolina to be near Cheryl's family.

With two small children and a third on the way, she began pursuing her real estate career. After a short time in residential sales, commercial and land sales became more her passion, and so her success in brokering land deals and managing properties began.

Cheryl resides in the small town of Wesley Chapel near Charlotte, North Carolina on family land near her parents. She feels blessed to have three healthy, happy children. She is so proud that both of her sons have earned the rank of Eagle Scout. One now has a dual engineering degree, and the other is a US Marine Reservist and auto mechanic. Her daughter is pursuing a career in the dental/medical field.

Even with a busy schedule as a single mother, Cheryl continues to grow and develop her real estate business while still making time for an array of hobbies and interests—such as shagging (the dance of the Carolinas), spartan races, skydiving, and small triathlons, as well as writing and painting ... just to name a few. She even still finds time to cut hair!

Above all else, she is a grateful follower and believer in her Lord and Savior, Jesus Christ.

Endnotes

1 Mandy Hale, *The Single Woman: Life, Love, and a Dash of Sass,* (Nashville, Tennessee: Thomas Nelson, 2013).

2 Bill Gallagher, "Bill Gallagher: Superior School of Real Estate," April 26, 2019, in *Welcome Home Lake Norman (LKN),* produced by Ryan Webber, podcast, MP3 audio, https://radiopublic.com/welcome-home-lkn-6VDQOl/s1!73b3a.

3 Sara Blakely, quoted in Peter Economy, The Leadership Guy, "Sara Blakely's Most Inspiring Quotes for Success," *Inc.* Magazine Online, updated March 20, 2015, https://www.inc.com/peter-economy/sara-blakely-19-inspiring-power-quotes-for-success.html.

4 Arthur H. Barnhisel, 1924, Preamble for the *Code of Ethics,* The National Association of Real Estate Exchanges, 1913.

5 Pamela Ann Sexton, "What Is a Geographic Information System (GIS)?" United States Geological Survey, n.d., https://www.usgs.gov/faqs/what-a-geographic-information-system-gis?qt-news_science_products=0#qt-news_science_products.

6 Cynthia Maybry and Anthony Merrell, email message to author, November 6, 2019.

7 GIS Geography, "What Is Topography? The Definitive Guide," updated July 30, 2020, https://gisgeography.com/what-is-topography/.

8 Jim Rohn, "Rohn: 4 Straightforward Steps to Success," *Success* Magazine Online, updated March 31, 2015.

9 Henry David Thoreau and H. Daniel Peck, *A Year in Thoreau's Journal: 1851,* (New York: Penguin Classics, 1993).

10 Marvin Phillips, *Never Lick a Moving Blender!* (New York: Howard Books, 1996).

11 Albert Einstein, quoted in Andrew Thomas, "20 Inspiring Quotes from the Most Successful People," *Inc.* Magazine Online, updated September 30, 2018, https://www.inc.com/anna-meyer/holiday-retail-shopping-trends-2020.html.

12 Margaret Mitchell, *Gone with the Wind,* (New York: MacMillan Company, 1936).

13 Theodore Roosevelt, *Theodore Roosevelt on Bravery: Lessons from the Most Courageous Leader of the Twentieth Century,* (New York: Skyhorse, 2015), 5.

14 Margaret Reiter, Attorney, "What Is a Property Lien? Learn What a Property Lien Is and How It Affects Your Property," Nolo, Legal Topics, n.d., https://www.nolo.com/legal-encyclopedia/what-property-lien.html.

15 Janet Wickell, "Residential Real Estate Appraisals." The Balance, updated June 5, 2020, https://www.thebalance.com/facts-about-residential-real-estate-appraisals-1797691.

16 Matt Sailor, "10 Deed Restrictions that Could Ruin Your Dream Home," How Stuff Works, n.d., https://home.howstuffworks.com/real-estate/buying-home/10-deed-restrictions.htm.

17 Doug Ruhlin, "What Is a Phase 1 Environmental Assessment?" Resource Management Associates (blog), n.d., https://www.rmagreen.com/rma-blog/what-is-a-phase-i-environmental-site-assessment.

18 Wikipedia, 2020, "Skyway," updated June 5, 2020, https://en.wikipedia.org/wiki/Skyway.

19 Bridge Brothers, "Skyway Bridges," n.d., https://bridgebrothers.com/skyway-bridges/.

20 Deeds.com, "All I Deed Is the Air I Breath" [sic], updated September 14, 2018, https://www.deeds.com/articles/all-i-deed-is-the-air-i-breath/.

21 Tech Target, "Drone (UAV)," Internet of Things Agenda, updated July, 2019, https://internetofthingsagenda.techtarget.com/definition/drone.

22 Federal Emergency Management Agency, "Flood Insurance," FEMA.gov, updated July 28, 2020, https://www.fema.gov/flood-insurance.

23 Lake Superior Duluth Streams, "Impervious Surfaces Hinder Infiltration and Increase Runoff," n.d., https://www.lakesuperiorstreams.org/understanding/impact_impervious.html.

24 Center for Watershed Protection, "Trees and Stormwater Runoff," updated, September 11, 2017, https://www.cwp.org/reducing-stormwater-runoff/.

25 Karen Cappiella, Tom Schueler, and Tiffany Wright, *Urban Watershed Forestry Manual: Part 2. Conserving and Planting Trees at Development Sites,* (Newton Square, Pennsylvania: United States Department of Agriculture Forest Service, 2006).

26 Amit Kalantri, ca. [2014?].

27 Find Law, "What Are Property Deeds?" Reviewed by Bridget Molitor, JD, updated May 12, 2020, https://realestate.findlaw.com/buying-a-home/what-are-property-deeds.html.

28 Shala Munroe, "Who Is Responsible for Preparing a Real Estate Deed?" PocketSense, Updated July 27, 2017, https://pocketsense.com/responsible-preparing-real-estate-deed-12300935.html.

29 Jean Folger, "Understanding Property Deeds," Investopedia, Real Estate Investing, Real Estate Investing Guide, updated, March 27, 2019. https://www.investopedia.com/articles/realestate/12/property-deeds-and-real-property.asp.

30 Rocket Lawyer, "What Is a Deed of Trust? Definition and How It Works," n.d., https://www.rocketlawyer.com/article/what-is-a-deed-of-trust-ps.rl.

31 Sandy Gadow, "What Is the Difference Between a Mortgage and a Deed of Trust?" SandyGadow.com, n.d., https://sandygadow.com/what-is-the-difference-between-a-mortgage-and-a-deed-of-trust/.

32 Wikipedia, 2020, "Quitclaim Deed," Updated July 18, 2020, https://en.wikipedia.org/wiki/Quitclaim_deed.

33 Deeds.com, "Quitclaim Deed," updated January 27, 2020, https://www.deeds.com/quit-claim-deed/.

34 Wikipedia, 2020, "Warranty Deed," updated November 25, 2019, https://en.wikipedia.org/wiki/Warranty_deed.

35 Justin T. Rush, "What Is a Correction Deed?" Legal Beagle, n.d., https://legalbeagle.com/6241488-scriveners-affidavit.html.

36 Julie Garber, "How to Use TOD or Beneficiary Deeds to Avoid Probate," The Balance, updated May 15, 2020, https://www.thebalance.com/use-deeds-avoid-probate-3505250.

37 Julie Kagan, "Special Warranty Deed Definition," Investopedia, updated July 19, 2020, https://www.investopedia.com/terms/s/special-warranty-deed.asp.

38 Carl W. Buehner, quoted in Richard Evans, *Richard Evans' Quote Book,* (1st ed.), (Salt Lake City: Publishers Press, 1971).

39 Daniel J. Rice, *Awake in the World: A Riverfeet Press Anthology,* (Bozeman, Montana: Riverfeet Press, 2017).

40 Land Century, "What Is Land Surveying and What Is It Used For?" updated February 26, 2018, https://www.landcentury.com/articles-news/what-is-land-surveying-and-what-is-it-used-for.

41 Lisa Kaplan Gordon, "What Is a Plat Map? A Survey that Can Tell You a Lot About Your Property," Realtor.com, updated December 10, 2019. https://www.realtor.com/advice/buy/what-is-a-plat-map/.

42 Todd Ewing, "Understanding 4 Types of Property Surveys," Federal Title and Escrow Company (blog), updated July 12, 2013, https://www.federaltitle.com/understanding-4-types-of-property-surveys/.

43 Tim Bowes, PLS Geomatics Manager and 2019 President North Carolina Society of Surveyors, email message to author, October 29, 2019.

44 Gary S. Kent, PLS, "ALTA/NSPS Standards," National Society of Professional Surveyors, n.d., https://www.nsps.us.com/page/ALTANSPSStandards.

45 North Carolina Society of Surveyors, "Protecting Your Biggest Investment," NC Surveyors, n.d., http://ncsurveyors.com/files/PDFs/Protecting%20Your%20Biggest%20Investment%20-%20Watermark.pdf.

46 Tim Bowes, ibid.

47 Jack Dickson, *Jerusalem Falls,* (Ridley Park: Ridley Park Books, 2012).

48 Reverend H.K. Williams, quoted in Charles Clay Doyle, Wolfgang Mieder, and Fred R. Shapiro, The Dictionary of Modern Proverbs, (New Haven: Connecticut, 2012).

49 Ingolf Vogeler, "What Is Zoning?" University of Wisconsin Eau Claire, n.d., https://people.uwec.edu/ivogeler/w270/what_is_zoning.htm.

50 Individual Rights and Government Wrongs, "Zoning Versus Deed Restrictions," Property, n.d., https://individualrightsgovernmentwrongs.com/property/zoning-versus-deed-restrictions/.

51 Law Shelf Educational Media, "Zoning Laws," National Paralegal College, n.d., https://lawshelf.com/coursewarecontentview/zoning-laws/.

52 Deeds.com, "What Are Deed Restrictions?" updated August 11, 2015, https://www.deeds.com/articles/what-are-deed-restrictions/.

53 Albert Szent-Györgyi, ca. [1960-1970?].

54 Seth Williams, "What the Heck Is a 'Perk Test' (and How Much Does It Really Matter)?" R.E. Tipster (blog), n.d., https://retipster.com/perc-test/.

55 Dr. Simon Ghanat, quoted in The Citadel, "Why Is Pluff Mud Smelly and Can It Be Stabilized? Civil Engineering Undergrad Researchers Look for Answers," Campus Life, Engineering, Featured, Students, August 23, 2019, https://today.citadel.edu/why-is-pluff-mud-smelly-and-can-it-be-stabilized-civil-engineering-undergrad-researchers-look-for-answers/.

56 Daily and Woods, PLLC, "What Is a Mineral Title Opinion?" (blog), n.d., http://www.dailywoods.com/blog/what-is-a-mineral-title-opinion.

57 Norman E. Hanson, "Abstracts and Oil Titles," *Montana Law Review,* vol. 17, no. 1, Fall 1955, 108–120. Rpt. in *The Scholarly Forum @ Montana Law,* University of Montana, https://scholarship.law.umt.edu/cgi/viewcontent.cgi?article=1255&context=mlr.

58 Janet Wickell, *The Everything Real Estate Investing Book: How to Get Started and Make the Most of Your Money,* (Avon, Massachusetts: Adams Media, 2004).

59 American Cancer Society, "Radon and Cancer," Sun and Other Types of Radiation, September 23, 2015, https://www.cancer.org/cancer/cancer-causes/radiation-exposure/radon.html.

60 United States Environmental Protection Agency, "EPA Map of Radon Zones," n.d., EPA.gov. n.d. https://www.epa.gov/sites/production/files/2015-07/documents/zonemapcolor.pdf.

61 Marilyn L. Rice, quoted in Goodreads, "Marilyn L. Rice Quotes," n.d., https://www.goodreads.com/author/quotes/3000920.Marilyn_L_Rice.

62 National Geographic, "All the water that will ever be is, right now," (quote) vol. 184, no. 4, October, 1993.

63 Three Oaks Engineering, "Types of Septic Systems," n.d., http://www.threeoaksengineering.com/types-of-septic-systems.html.

64 Albert Einstein, quoted in Alice Calaprice, *The Quotable Einstein,* (Princeton, New Jersey: Princeton University Press, 1996).

65 Abraham Lincoln, quoted in Arnold Kunst, *Lincoln 365: A Primer in Patriotism as Lived* by Abraham Lincoln, (Scotts Valley, California: Create Space Independent Publishing Platform, 2011).

66 Wikipedia, 2020, "Homeowner Association," updated May 31, 2020, https://en.wikipedia.org/wiki/Homeowner_association

67 Red Fin, "What Are Covenants, Conditions, and Restrictions (CC&Rs)?" Real Estate Glossary, n.d., https://www.redfin.com/definition/covenants-conditions-restrictions.

68 Spectrum Association Management (blog), "How to Find Your CC&Rs," n.d., https://spectrumam.com/how-to-find-your-ccrs/.

69 George Herman "Babe" Ruth, quoted in Barney Cotton, "How to Beat a Sales Slump," *Business Insider UK,* July 31, 2018, https://www.businessleader.co.uk/how-to-beat-a-sales-slump/49069/.

70 Beth Ross, "When HOA Associations Can Impose Special Assessments: Learning to Expect and Predict Financial Surprises," Nolo, Legal Topics, n.d., https://www.nolo.com/legal-encyclopedia/homeowners-association/when-hoa-associations-can-impose-special-assessments.html.

71 Zig Ziglar, *Zig Ziglar's Secrets of Closing the Sale: For Anyone Who Must Get Others to Say Yes!* (reissue ed.), (New York: Berkley, 1985).

72 Jessie Potter, quoted in Tom Ahern, "Search for Quality Called Key to Life," *The Milwaukee Sentinel,* Column 5, October 24, 1981, 5.

73 Jim Rohn, *My Philosophy for Successful Living,* (Melrose, Florida: No Dream Too Big, LLC, 2012).

74 Henry Ford, *The Reader's Digest,* Quote Page (Filler item), Volume 51, 64.

75 Lewis Carroll, quoted in Robert Glazer, "Regretting Our Regrets," Friday Forward (blog), #41, October 14, 2016, https://www.robertglazer.com/friday-forward/regretting-regrets/.

Bibliography

American Cancer Society. "Radon and Cancer." Sun and Other Types of Radiation. September 23, 2015. https://www.cancer.org/cancer/cancer-causes/radiation-exposure/radon.html.

Barnhisel, Arthur H. 1924. Preamble for the *Code of Ethics*. The National Association of Real Estate Exchanges, 1913.

Blakely, Sara. Quoted in Peter Economy, The Leadership Guy. "Sara Blakely's Most Inspiring Quotes for Success." Inc. Magazine Online. Updated March 20, 2015. https://www.inc.com/peter-economy/sara-blakely-19-inspiring-power-quotes-for-success.html.

Bowes, Tim, PLS Geomatics Manager and 2019 President North Carolina Society of Surveyors. Email message to author. October 29, 2019.

Bridge Brothers. "Skyway Bridges." n.d. https://bridgebrothers.com/skyway-bridges/.

Buehner, Carl W. Quoted in Richard Evans, *Richard Evans' Quote Book*. (1st ed.) Salt Lake City: Publishers Press, 1971.

Cappiella, Karen, Tom Schueler, and Tiffany Wright. *Urban Watershed Forestry Manual: Part 2. Conserving and Planting Trees at Development Sites*. Newton Square, Pennsylvania: United States Department of Agriculture Forest Service, 2006.

Carroll, Lewis. Quoted in Robert Glazer, "Regretting Our Regrets." Friday Forward (blog), #41. October 14, 2016. https://www.robertglazer.com/friday-forward/regretting-regrets/.

Center for Watershed Protection. "Trees and Stormwater Runoff." Updated, September 11, 2017. https://www.cwp.org/reducing-stormwater-runoff/.

Daily and Woods, PLLC. "What Is a Mineral Title Opinion?" (blog). n.d. http://www.dailywoods.com/blog/what-is-a-mineral-title-opinion.

Deeds.com. "All I Deed Is the Air I Breath. [sic] Updated September 14, 2018. https://www.deeds.com/articles/all-i-deed-is-the-air-i-breath/.

Deeds.com. "Quitclaim Deed." Updated January 27, 2020. https://www.deeds.com/quit-claim-deed/.

Deeds.com. "What Are Deed Restrictions?" Updated August 11, 2015. https://www.deeds.com/articles/what-are-deed-restrictions/.

Dickson, Jack. *Jerusalem Falls*. Ridley Park: Ridley Park Books, 2012.

Einstein, Albert. Quoted in Alice Calaprice, *The Quotable Einstein*. Princeton, New Jersey: Princeton University Press, 1996.

Einstein, Albert. Quoted in Andrew Thomas, "20 Inspiring Quotes from the Most Successful People." *Inc.* Magazine Online. September 30, 2018. https://www.inc.com/anna-meyer/holiday-retail-shopping-trends-2020.html.

Ewing, Todd. "Understanding 4 Types of Property Surveys." Federal Title and Escrow Company (blog). Updated July 12, 2013. https://www.federaltitle.com/understanding-4-types-of-property-surveys/.

Federal Emergency Management Agency. "Flood Insurance." FEMA.gov. Updated July 28, 2020. https://www.fema.gov/flood-insurance.

Find Law. "What Are Property Deeds?" Reviewed by Bridget Molitor, JD. Updated May 12, 2020. https://realestate.findlaw.com/buying-a-home/what-are-property-deeds.html.

Folger, Jean. "Understanding Property Deeds." Investopedia. Real Estate Investing, Real Estate Investing Guide. Updated, March 27, 2019. https://www.investopedia.com/articles/realestate/12/property-deeds-and-real-property.asp.

Ford, Henry. *The Reader's Digest.* Quote Page (Filler item). Volume 51. 64.

Gadow, Sandy. "What Is the Difference Between a Mortgage and a Deed of Trust?" SandyGadow.com. n.d. https://sandygadow.com/what-is-the-difference-between-a-mortgage-and-a-deed-of-trust/.

Gallagher, Bill. "Bill Gallagher: Superior School of Real Estate." April 26, 2019. Produced by Ryan Webber, podcast, MP3 audio. *Welcome Home Lake Norman (LKN).* https://radiopublic.com/welcome-home-lkn-6VDQOl/s1!73b3a.

Garber, Julie. "How to Use TOD or Beneficiary Deeds to Avoid Probate." The Balance. Updated May 15, 2020. https://www.thebalance.com/use-deeds-avoid-probate-3505250.

Ghanat, Dr. Simon. Quoted in The Citadel, "Why Is Pluff Mud Smelly and Can It Be Stabilized? Civil Engineering Undergrad Researchers Look for Answers." Campus Life, Engineering, Featured, Students. August 23, 2019. https://today.citadel.edu/why-is-pluff-mud-smelly-and-can-it-be-stabilized-civil-engineering-undergrad-researchers-look-for-answers/.

GIS Geography. "What Is Topography? The Definitive Guide." Updated July 30, 2020. https://gisgeography.com/what-is-topography/.

Gordon, Lisa Kaplan. "What Is a Plat Map? A Survey that Can Tell You a Lot About Your Property." Realtor.com. Updated December 10, 2019. https://www.realtor.com/advice/buy/what-is-a-plat-map/.

Hale, Mandy. *The Single Woman: Life, Love, and a Dash of Sass.* Nashville, Tennessee: Thomas Nelson, 2013.

Hanson, Norman E. "Abstracts and Oil Titles." *Montana Law Review.* vol. 17, no. 1. Fall 1955. 108–120. Rpt. in *The Scholarly Forum @ Montana Law.* University of Montana. https://scholarship.law.umt.edu/cgi/viewcontent.cgi?article=1255&context=mlr.

Individual Rights and Government Wrongs. "Zoning Versus Deed Restrictions." Property. n.d. https://individualrightsgovernmentwrongs.com/property/zoning-versus-deed-restrictions/.

Kagan, Julie. "Special Warranty Deed Definition." Investopedia. Updated July 19, 2020. https://www.investopedia.com/terms/s/special-warranty-deed.asp.

Kalantri, Amit. ca. [2014?].

Kent, Gary S., PLS. "ALTA/NSPS Standards." National Society of Professional Surveyors. n.d. https://www.nsps.us.com/page/ALTANSPSStandards.

Lake Superior Duluth Streams. "Impervious Surfaces Hinder Infiltration and Increase Runoff." n.d. https://www.lakesuperiorstreams.org/understanding/impact_impervious.html.

Land Century. "What Is Land Surveying and What Is It Used For?" Updated February 26, 2018. https://www.landcentury.com/articles-news/what-is-land-surveying-and-what-is-it-used-for.

Law Shelf Educational Media. "Zoning Laws." National Paralegal College. n.d. https://lawshelf.com/coursewarecontentview/zoning-laws/.

Lincoln, Abraham. Quoted in Arnold Kunst, Lincoln 365: *A Primer in Patriotism as Lived by Abraham Lincoln.* Scotts Valley, California: Create Space Independent Publishing Platform, 2011.

Maybry, Cynthia and Anthony Merrell. Email message to author. November 6, 2019.

Mitchell, Margaret. *Gone with the Wind.* New York: MacMillan Company, 1936.

Munroe, Shala. "Who Is Responsible for Preparing a Real Estate Deed?" PocketSense. Updated July 27, 2017. https://pocketsense.com/responsible-preparing-real-estate-deed-12300935.html.

National Geographic. "All the water that will ever be is, right now." (quote) vol. 184., no. 4. October, 1993.

North Carolina Society of Surveyors. "Protecting Your Biggest Investment." NC Surveyors. n.d. http://ncsurveyors.com/files/PDFs/Protecting%20Your%20Biggest%20Investment%20-%20Watermark.pdf.

Phillips, Marvin. *Never Lick a Moving Blender!* New York: Howard Books, 1996.

Potter, Jessie. Quoted in Tom Ahern, "Search for Quality Called Key to Life." *The Milwaukee Sentinel.* Column 5. October 24, 1981, 5.

Red Fin. "What Are Covenants, Conditions, and Restrictions (CC&Rs)?" Real Estate Glossary. n.d. https://www.redfin.com/definition/covenants-conditions-restrictions.

Reiter, Margaret, Attorney. "What Is a Property Lien? Learn What a Property Lien Is and How It Affects Your Property." Nolo. Legal Topics. n.d. https://www.nolo.com/legal-encyclopedia/what-property-lien.html.

Rice, Daniel J. *Awake in the World: A Riverfeet Press Anthology*. Bozeman, Montana: Riverfeet Press, 2017.

Rice, Marilyn L. Quoted in Goodreads, "Marilyn L. Rice Quotes." n.d. https://www.goodreads.com/author/quotes/3000920.Marilyn_L_Rice.

Rocket Lawyer. "What Is a Deed of Trust? Definition and How It Works." n.d. https://www.rocketlawyer.com/article/what-is-a-deed-of-trust-ps.rl.

Rohn, Jim. *My Philosophy for Successful Living*. Melrose, Florida: No Dream Too Big, LLC, 2012.

Rohn, Jim. "Rohn: 4 Straightforward Steps to Success." *Success* Magazine Online. March 31, 2015.

Roosevelt, Theodore. *Theodore Roosevelt on Bravery: Lessons from the Most Courageous Leader of the Twentieth Century*. New York: Skyhorse, 2015, 5.

Ross, Beth. "When HOA Associations Can Impose Special Assessments: Learning to Expect and Predict Financial Surprises." Nolo. Legal Topics. n.d. https://www.nolo.com/legal-encyclopedia/homeowners-association/when-hoa-associations-can-impose-special-assessments.html.

Ruhlin, Doug. "What Is a Phase 1 Environmental Assessment?" Resource Management Associates (blog). n.d. https://www.rmagreen.com/rma-blog/what-is-a-phase-i-environmental-site-assessment.

Rush, Justin T. "What Is a Correction Deed?" Legal Beagle. n.d. https://legalbeagle.com/6241488-scriveners-affidavit.html.

Ruth, George Herman "Babe." Quoted in Barney Cotton, "How to Beat a Sales Slump." *Business Insider UK*. July 31, 2018. https://www.businessleader.co.uk/how-to-beat-a-sales-slump/49069/.

Sailor, Matt. "10 Deed Restrictions that Could Ruin Your Dream Home." How Stuff Works. n.d. https://home.howstuffworks.com/real-estate/buying-home/10-deed-restrictions.htm.

Sexton, Pamela Ann. "What Is a Geographic Information System (GIS)?" United States Geological Survey. n.d. https://www.usgs.gov/faqs/what-a-geographic-information-system-gis?qt-news_science_products=0#qt-news_science_products.

Spectrum Association Management (blog). "How to Find Your CC&Rs." n.d. https://spectrumam.com/how-to-find-your-ccrs/.

Szent-Györgyi, Albert. ca. [1960-1970?].

Tech Target. "Drone (UAV)." Internet of Things Agenda. Updated July, 2019. https://internetofthingsagenda.techtarget.com/definition/drone.

Three Oaks Engineering. "Types of Septic Systems." n.d. http://www.threeoaksengineering.com/types-of-septic-systems.html.

Thoreau, Henry David, and H. Daniel Peck. *A Year in Thoreau's Journal: 1851*. New York: Penguin Classics, 1993.

United States Environmental Protection Agency. "EPA Map of Radon Zones." EPA.gov. n.d. https://www.epa.gov/sites/production/files/2015-07/documents/zonemapcolor.pdf.

Vogeler, Ingolf. "What Is Zoning?" University of Wisconsin Eau Claire. n.d. https://people.uwec.edu/ivogeler/w270/what_is_zoning.htm

Wickell, Janet. *The Everything Real Estate Investing Book: How to Get Started and Make the Most of Your Money*. Avon, Massachusetts: Adams Media, 2004.

Wickell, Janet. "Residential Real Estate Appraisals." The Balance. Updated June 5, 2020. https://www.thebalance.com/facts-about-residential-real-estate-appraisals-1797691.

Wikipedia. 2020. "Homeowner Association." Updated May 31, 2020. https://en.wikipedia.org/wiki/Homeowner_association

Wikipedia. 2020. "Quitclaim Deed." Updated July 18, 2020. https://en.wikipedia.org/wiki/Quitclaim_deed.

Wikipedia. 2020. "Skyway." Updated June 5, 2020. https://en.wikipedia.org/wiki/Skyway.

Wikipedia. 2020. "Warranty Deed." n.d. https://en.wikipedia.org/wiki/Warranty_deed.

Williams, Reverend H.K. Quoted in Charles Clay Doyle, Wolfgang Mieder, and Fred R. Shapiro, *The Dictionary of Modern Proverbs*. New Haven: Connecticut, 2012.

Williams, Seth. "What the Heck Is a 'Perk Test' (and How Much Does It Really Matter)?" R.E. Tipster (blog). n.d. https://retipster.com/perc-test/.

Ziglar, Zig. *Zig Ziglar's Secrets of Closing the Sale: For Anyone Who Must Get Others to Say Yes!* (reissue ed.) New York: Berkley, 1985.

CPSIA information can be obtained
at www.ICGtesting.com
Printed in the USA
BVHW071509230122
626881BV00004B/62